AMERICANS BY ADOPTION

L. Agassiz

AMERICANS BY ADOPTION

BRIEF BIOGRAPHIES OF
GREAT CITIZENS BORN IN
FOREIGN LANDS

By JOSEPH HUSBAND

WITH AN INTRODUCTION BY
WILLIAM ALLAN NEILSON

ILLUSTRATED

Essay Index Reprint Series

 BOOKS FOR LIBRARIES PRESS
FREEPORT, NEW YORK

First Published **1920**

Reprinted 1969

STANDARD BOOK NUMBER:

8369-1142-3

LIBRARY OF CONGRESS CATALOG CARD NUMBER:

70-86763

PRINTED IN THE UNITED STATES OF AMERICA

To

EDWARD F. SANDERSON

CONTENTS

LIST OF ILLUSTRATIONS

INTRODUCTION

THERE is an old story, told in many countries through the Middle Ages, of a knight who got into trouble, and was offered pardon if within a year he brought the correct answer to the question, "What do women most desire?" At the last moment he saved himself by answering, "Their own way," or words to that effect.

This is a man's story, and scores the man's point in the perennial strife of wits between the sexes; but the answer needs but little modification to hold good of men and women alike. When one takes up a book like this, dealing with the lives of men who deliberately and voluntarily left the homes of their fathers to become citizens of a strange land, one naturally asks what they wanted, and equally naturally goes on to ask what men in general want most in life.

Many answers have been given to the question, and none can be final, because men and circumstances differ so widely. But I should like to propose one that seems to me of more general application than most. Men want most to count among their fellows for what they are worth. This desire is more persistent than love, more universal than the thirst for wealth or power, more fundamental than the demand for pleasure. It shows itself in early childhood, it steers the ambitions of manhood, its fulfillment is the crown of old age. The degree of the chance to achieve it is the measure of the desirability of a country as a place to live in; and it is fair to say that the men whose lives are told in this book, and we others who have come to America of our own accord, have done so because we believed that these United States, above all countries of the world, give men this chance to make the most of themselves.

"To count among their fellows for what they are worth" — see what this implies. First, and most superficially, it means recognition of ability and character by society. Carried to the highest point, it would mean the absence of handicaps, of privilege, of "pull" — the equality of opportunity for achieving distinction which has always been the theory of this democracy. Of course, neither here nor elsewhere is this perfect condition reached; but the biographies in this book tend to show that there has long been a large degree of it here, and our social progress has this condition frankly accepted as a goal.

Secondly, it implies a basis for self-respect. Deeper than the grudge that a man has against the society which refuses him due credit for his achievement is the grudge that a man feels when he has to admit to himself that his achievement is not really creditable. The worst curse of slavery was not its external restrictions, but its effect in crushing the slave's sense of the potential nobility of his own soul. The feeling that a man has a fair chance to be taken at his full value is an exhilarating feeling, liberating his powers, freeing him from the gnawing pains of mortified vanity, impelling him to hold his head up and look his neighbor in the eye.

Thirdly, it means a chance to do one's job — one's own job — and to do it to the limit of one's capacity. This is the foundation on which both recognition and self-respect must be built. "Blessed is the man," says Carlyle, "who has found his work; let him seek no other blessedness." Because a man is freer in America to pass from one calling to another, from one class to another, from one region to another; because here people are willing to be shown what he can do; the chances are greater than elsewhere that he will find the task and circumstances which fit him best and let him count for most.

If you read through these nine lives, you will see that what each of these men was really after, and what each found more fully here than in the old world, was not wealth or power or pleasure of the senses, but the chance to do the biggest job of which he was capable. Three of them, indeed, did gather great wealth, but it was either a by-product of the main achievement of their lives, or the instrument of that achievement. The vision that inspired James J. Hill was not a colossal fortune, but the opening up and populating of a great territory with farmers leading large, wholesome, and prosperous lives. Two of the nine were artists, who neither asked nor received great financial rewards, but who found here the chance to create beauty and to form taste, and in seizing this chance they found their supreme satisfaction.

Of these nine men I have known only one, Augustus Saint-Gaudens; but none could have illustrated better the spirit in which work has to be done if it is to yield its greatest reward. What struck me in watching Saint-Gaudens work was his absolute indifference to what a statue would cost him in pains or in time, or to what it would bring him in money, and his complete absorption in making it as nearly perfect as he could. He did not "count the mortal years it takes to mould the immortal forms." He would work for hours on the modeling of an inch of surface, seeking for an exactness of result imperceptible to the lay bystander. He would never be hurried — and he found America willing to wait.

The same spirit worked in Ericsson in his inventions, in Carl Schurz in his unceasing quest for political justice, in Riis in his cleaning up of New York City. Some of these men were not outstanding intellects, but each cared intensely about his job, and to each America gave his chance.

I have a quarrel with the title of this book. "Americans by Choice" it should be, not "Americans by Adoption." "Adoption" suggests that America adopt us. We who have of our own accord left the old world and taken up citizenship in the new know that we have chosen her, not she us. We can leave to the native-born their natural pride in their birthright, but we can claim that we pay a greater compliment to this land than can these others, for our citizenship is not the result of an accident but of our free choice. And we have paid our price. We, and we alone, know what it has cost to leave behind scenes and traditions and affections which clung close to the heart. But that we have left them is proof that we prized still more highly the opportunity that America offered us to count for what we are worth.

In the face of this proof we have no apologies to make. We call our nine worthies to witness; and, while not forgetting our due of gratitude for our chance, we point to the use we make of the chance, and ask the native-born to acknowledge that the balance swings level. More than this we cannot ask; less than this we will not take. Granted this, without grudging and without condescension, we can quiet all fears of divided allegiance, and work with our fellow citizens for the perfecting of the social order in which these wise and worthy men found an environment for accomplishment of the first rank, and with which we have thrown in our lot in becoming Americans by choice.

W. A. NEILSON.

NORTHAMPTON, MASSACHUSETTS
    MARCH, 1920

AMERICANS BY ADOPTION

I

STEPHEN GIRARD

Born in Bordeaux, France, 1750
Died in Philadelphia, 1831

THE old French city of Bordeaux has for centuries been one of the greatest maritime cities of Europe. Situated on the low shore of the River Garonne, its stone quays have for generations been close-packed with the ships of a world-wide commerce. Under the Roman Empire it was a flourishing city; in the fourth century, surrounded by massive walls and lofty towers, it became the capital of Aquitania Secunda; and later, for three hundred years, it was ruled by English kings. Here reigned Edward, the Black Prince, and here was born his son Richard. Between the Bordeaux merchants and the English an extensive commerce developed, and as years passed by, this commerce branched out into a world-activity that to-day maintains relations with all civilized lands, but chiefly, as has been the case for a century and a half, with England, South America, the West Indies, and the United States.

In the year 1750 the stone wharves along the river bristled with the masts and spars of the fleets of the Bordeaux merchants. Small ships they were compared with the great steel cargo-carriers that to-day line the stream; but they were staunchly built and strongly manned, and their rich cargoes, safely transported from the distant Indies, filled the city with wealth and the romance of blue salt water and foreign lands.

In that same year, in a house in rue Ramonet au Chartrons, then a suburb of the city, was born Stephen Girard, son of Pierre Girard, Captain of the Port of Bordeaux. Pierre the father was a man of some importance and a prosperous merchant in the city. In 1744, during the War of the Austrian Succession, he had served with honor in the French navy, and at the blockade of Brest, he had received the Military Order of Saint Louis for his heroic action in putting out the flames on his ship, which had been fired by a fire-ship sent into the French squadron by the British. In later years he became Burgess of Bordeaux, and during this period he began to trade with the French ports in the island of San Domingo in the West Indies. Of such stock was the boy Stephen; born with the romance of the sea as his inheritance and with the heroic memory of his father to inspire him, but born with a handicap which, however, he never permitted to retard his progress; for from birth he was sightless in his right eye.

It was natural that the boy should turn to the sea. When he was twelve years old, the death of his mother left him a half-orphan. His education had been of the most general nature. There was little to draw him into the occupations of the land. To the lonesome lad the sea offered at least the promise of adventure, and perhaps the rewards of wealth and distinction. In the year 1764 Stephen was fourteen. His father's trading activities with the West Indies afforded the opening he desired; and with his few belongings packed in a sea-chest, he shipped as cabin-boy on a small merchantman to Port-au-Prince. Five more voyages followed, and in 1773 he was licensed to act as "captain, master, or pilot of any merchant ship he could obtain."

A year later as "officer of the ship" La Julie, he sailed from Bordeaux for Port-au-Prince. It was the final severance of his tie with France. The cargo consisted chiefly of general merchandise, in which Stephen had purchased a small share, bought from Bordeaux merchants with notes, or promises to pay at some later date. But business was slow in the islands, and the goods sold at a loss of over twenty-five per cent. In those days a man might be imprisoned for debt, and Girard realized that such a fate might await him should he return to Bordeaux. Accordingly, he obtained his discharge from the ship, and with a young acquaintance determined to form a partnership for the purpose of trading between the island ports. So with many who have sought freedom in the new world, cruel laws and the dread of an unjust imprisonment forced Girard to forsake his native land. But the just debt which he owed was not forgotten, and in later years the Bordeaux merchants, whose anger he had feared, received from him payment in full of the merchandise they had advanced him.

In July, 1774, Girard sailed for New York with a small cargo of coffee and sugar. It was a stirring time in the history of the American Colonies. For a dozen years the free spirit of the Americans had chafed under the oppression of British rule. Open fighting had occurred in Boston in 1770, when, in a fight between the populace and the British soldiers, three men were killed and eight were wounded. Two years later the British revenue schooner Gaspee was seized and burned by the people of Rhode Island, and in 1773 the citizens of Boston, disguised as Indians, emptied into the water of Boston Harbor 342 chests of tea from an English merchantman, as a protest against taxation without representation in Parliament. In retaliation, acts obnoxious to the people of Massachusetts were passed by the British Government; and in answer to these, on September 5, 1774, the Continental Congress was assembled at Philadelphia, and a declaration of rights was drawn up and published, defining the spirit of the American Colonies and indicating the consequences which must follow further interference with the liberty of the American people to levy their own taxes and make their own laws in their own Colonial assemblies.

Backing words with deeds, the Colony of Massachusetts set up its own government in defiance of General Gage, the British representative, and placed at its head John Hancock, an influential merchant of Boston. Twelve thousand volunteer militiamen were organized, — of whom about one third were known as "minute men," or soldiers ready to march or fight at a minute's notice, — and stores and ammunition were collected. Into such a scene sailed the young French boy with his cargo of sugar and coffee; and it is not surprising that his liberty-loving spirit sympathized with the indomitable determination of the colonists to rid themselves of the yoke of an old-world nation, and led him to seek employment in New York City, with some merchants there who traded with San Domingo.

First as mate and soon as captain, Girard steadily sailed back and forth between New York and the trading town of Le Cap in San Domingo. As captain of the little vessel, he was allowed by the owners the privilege of carrying a limited store of goods for his own venture, in addition to the regular cargo. His capital was small, but no opportunity to increase it was ever allowed to pass, and each voyage showed a steadily increasing profit to the credit of the youthful trader.

Meanwhile, in America, the fighting at Lexington and Concord had announced to the world the determination of the liberty-loving colonists to cast off British rule, and in 1775 the War of American Independence was begun. But important as this war is in American eyes, it was but one of several difficulties which confronted Great Britain: three years later war was begun between that country and France, and in 1779 Spain also declared war on Great Britain; this was followed in 1780 by the declaration of war between Great Britain and Holland.

Immediately all American shipping became subject

to seizure by British vessels, and accordingly Girard availed himself of the neutrality of France and shifted to the protection of the French flag. But the dangers of the sea, increased by the hazards of war, were enormous, and in 1776 Girard found himself practically shipwrecked off the Delaware coast. With difficulty he brought his ship to shore, and soon found himself in the little city of Philadelphia, which was destined in after years to claim him as its foremost citizen.

Philadelphia was a town of twenty-four thousand inhabitants. By slow-sailing packets its people kept uncertain contact with the news of the old-world cities; stage coach and post-rider kept them informed of home affairs. A few small newspapers reported the stirring events then occurring. But Girard was not particularly concerned with the struggle of the American Colonies. He was still a Frenchman trading with the West Indies, concerned only with his ships, his markets, and his fortune. Philadelphia seemed to him to be an enterprising and growing place, and accordingly he settled there. It was perhaps the most important decision in his life.

As he was forced by the presence of British war vessels off the coast to abandon his trading ventures with the West Indies, Girard's activities were for two years limited to local affairs. During the blockade an event took place which gave him a real tie with the struggling states: he married an American, Miss Mary Lum. In 1778 the British forces occupied Philadelphia and seized the Water Witch, the first vessel owned entirely by the enterprising Frenchman.

Philadelphia, however, was soon again in American hands, and the sea communication for foreign trade was restored. With the reopening of commerce Girard formed a partnership with his brother, who was now living at Le Cap, for the purpose of trading between Le Cap and Philadelphia. Salt, syrup, sugar, and coffee were desired by the Americans, and by their importation he saw a "big profit."

Business prospered, and in 1779 Girard wrote to his father: "Tired of the risks of a sailor's life, I determined to settle ashore. . . . I have taken a wife who is without fortune, but whom I love and with whom I am living very happily. By hard work I have finished furnishing my house, increased my capital to thirty-five thousand and hope to make good all my past losses."

Peace came in 1783, and with it ports were reopened and trade resumed. Convinced that by owning his own vessels his profits on each trading voyage would be largely increased, Girard became the sole owner of a small brig, the Two Brothers, which was built by him for his particular purposes. It was the actual beginning of that mercantile career which was to make him in time the richest merchant in America. The Two Brothers sailed for Le Cap with a cargo of flour and lumber. The return cargo consisted of molasses, sugar, coffee, and soap. The profits each way were large, and a second voyage to Le Cap was promptly undertaken.

Meanwhile, Girard, realizing the opportunities which the new Republic promised, had become a citizen, taking the oath of allegiance at Philadelphia on the twenty-seventh of October, 1778. Among the first of the millions of old-world people who in the years which followed were destined to renounce the oppressive institutions of their native lands and become naturalized citizens of the free United States, it is particularly interesting that Girard was born in a country which likewise was soon to cast aside the rule of kings and establish the institutions of a republic.

From now on Girard's fortune seemed steadily to advance. In 1789 George Washington became the first President of the new Republic. With the cessation of war at home and abroad, commerce was again resumed, and an era of prosperity gave to such men as Stephen Girard the opportunity to reap richly of the world's commercial harvest.

Crop failures in France had created a demand for foreign wheat, and to stimulate its importation the French Government offered a premium to anyone importing it. It was an attractive speculation, and Girard, with his eye ever scanning world opportunities while others passed them by, saw his chance to turn an honest penny. Promptly his own ships and other chartered vessels were filled with grain, and an abundant profit was quickly realized.

In these early days, the yellow fever, now eradicated by modern knowledge of sanitation, took each year its death-toll among the inhabitants of southern countries, and from time to time extended far beyond its normal field. Girard, and, in fact, most of the American merchants of that day, had conducted a large business with San Domingo, the principal trading centre of the West Indies. In 1791, however, the large negro population of the island revolted, and fire, slaughter, and plunder soon turned the prosperous community into a wilderness. White refugees crowded every outgoing vessel and by the hundreds began to pour into Philadelphia and other American seaboard cities. "Take advantage of my brig Polly," wrote Girard to a friend on the unhappy island, "if she still be in the harbor, to come here and enjoy the peace which our Republican Government, founded as it is on the rights of man, assures to all its inhabitants."

But with the refugees came also the dreaded plague, and baffling the skill of the doctors, it spread through Philadelphia until the streets were crowded with funerals and the church-bells seemed continually to toll. There were few hospitals in those days, and the Philadelphia hospital at Bush Hill was not only crowded far beyond its capacity, but was in wretched condition, owing to the lack of attendants. Girard was put on a committee, and that very evening reported the immediate need of nurses and money. But Girard did not stop with his duties as committeeman. Without hesitation, and totally ignoring the probability of contracting the fever himself, he and a fellow townsman, Peter Helm, assumed active control of the hospital, and day and night, throughout the plague, toiled at this self-imposed work of mercy among the sick and the dying.

Among the various accounts of the plague the following is of particular interest in its mention of

Girard: "Stephen Girard, a French merchant long resident here, and Peter Helm, born here of German parents, men whose names and services should never be forgotten, had the humanity and courage constantly to attend the hospital, and not only saw that the nurses did their duties, but they actually performed many of the most dangerous, and at the same time humiliating services for the sick with their own hands."

When the plague was over, Girard returned to his business. In February, 1793, France declared war on Great Britain, and immediately British troops and ships seized the French cities in San Domingo. Ships of war and privateers of both countries promptly swarmed over the seas. Decrees were soon published by the nations at war, forbidding neutral vessels to trade with enemy ports. The law of nations was disregarded, and American ships were seized and confiscated. Great Britain particularly ignored the rights of American ship-owners, and thousands of dollars worth of American ships and cargoes were soon in British hands. Two of Girard's ships, the Kitty and the Sally, were taken. Commerce was demoralized.

In retaliation against the outrages perpetrated by the British and the French, a "non-intercourse bill" provided that after November 1, 1794, "all commercial intercourse between the citizens of the United States and the subjects of the King of Great Britain should cease." The bill was lost in the Senate, but an embargo which closed all American ports to foreign trade accomplished practically the same end. In all, five ships belonging to Girard were now in enemy hands.

In October, 1801, after eight years of war, peace was concluded between France and Great Britain, and in December the war which the United States had been conducting against France was also ended. With the return of peace came renewed commercial activity. Girard at once availed himself of the opportunity, and soon his ships were engaged in trade with the ports of France and Russia. But this revival of commerce was of short duration, for the unsettled state of Europe soon resulted in new blockades of ports, embargoes, and acts of non-intercourse against the offending countries. Then, to complete the disaster, in 1810 Napoleon annexed Holland to France and issued a decree "by which American ships and cargoes, seized in the ports of Holland, Spain, France, and Naples, to the value of ten million dollars, were condemned and sold." Five of Girard's ships which had sailed for northern ports were now seized and held by the Danes, and it was many months before their release could be secured. Trade with Europe was at an end; but despite the heavy losses which Girard had suffered, he did not hesitate or allow himself to be mastered by the situation. If Europe was closed, South America and the Far East were open to him, and now his ships began new commerce with new continents, and in December, 1810, the ship Montesquieu set sail for Valparaiso and Canton.

During these years of commercial activity Girard had become a large investor in real estate, and of his profits from his trading ventures at sea he had in 1812 almost four hundred thousand dollars invested in farm acres and lots and buildings in Philadelphia. In 1812 the United States declared war against Great Britain. Bad feeling had long existed, due primarily to the disregard of the British for the rights of American vessels. For a long time Great Britain persisted in stopping our ships, taking American seamen out of them and forcing them to serve on British vessels. It was more than patriotism could bear, and the nation enthusiastically entered the war with the cry of "Free Trade and Sailor's Rights." Forced practically from the sea, Girard turned his great abilities to finance and the service of his country.

Girard was now sixty-two years old, but age did not deter him from a new enterprise. A bank had long been needed in Philadelphia, and to take advantage of the opportunity, Girard established a banking institution with a capital of over a million dollars, which was called Stephen Girard's Bank. The cost of the war which was being fought with Great Britain was a severe strain on the finances of the United States, and at the close of the year 1812 it became necessary for the Treasury to borrow money or the nation would become bankrupt. Sixteen million dollars was all that was required, but the loan was a failure, and less than four millions was subscribed. In April a new offering of the loan was prepared, but again the effort to float it ended in failure. In all only $5,838,000 was subscribed. More than ten million dollars must still be borrowed.

Now came an opportunity for Girard to repay to the United States the debt of gratitude for all that his citizenship had brought him. To the United States he owed his all, for in this free and fearless country he had been enabled to amass his great fortune. With two other men of means, Girard came forward and offered to subscribe for the entire balance of the loan. The offer was promptly accepted, and a situation of great embarrassment to the country was avoided.

With the defeat of Napoleon at Leipsic in 1813, and his abdication in 1814, Great Britain found herself free to conduct a more strenuous attack on the United States, and for a time matters went badly with the youthful nation. A British raid on the city of Washington resulted in the burning of the Capitol, the President's house, and other public buildings; and this was followed in September by a raid on Baltimore, which, however, resulted in failure. Great panic was caused by these actions, and for a time banking was demoralized and business practically suspended. But on Christmas Eve, 1814, a treaty of peace was signed at Ghent, and once more Girard promptly resumed his world-wide trading, and once more the Stars and Stripes blew free from halyards.

Girard suffered two severe losses by reason of the war, in the loss of his ship Good Friends and in a ransom of $180,000 which he was required to pay for his ship Montesquieu and cargo, captured while returning from Canton, China. But in spite of this, so greatly had his wealth increased, that he now paid more than a hundredth part of the total taxes of the city of

Philadelphia and his commercial capital was sufficient to enable him to sell goods on credit and to
carry on a maritime business throughout the world
without aid of discount. "All this," he has stated, "do
I owe principally to my close attention to business,
and to the resources which this fine country affords to
all active or industrious men."

In the years which followed, Girard found declining
profit in European cargoes brought to Philadelphia,
and in 1821 he began to trade heavily with the Far
East. Two of his ships, the Voltaire and the Montesquieu, were wrecked during this period; but Girard
was as good a loser as a gainer, and pocketed his
losses with small comment. Out of his fleet only four
ships remained. Girard was now an old man, markets
were bad owing to the panic in England and on the
Continent, and the prospect for continuous profitable
trading seemed ominous. It was only natural that he
should turn from the sea.

Speculation in land had proved to be as fascinating
as his speculations in ships and cargoes. Girard began
to buy land, and soon his total holdings amounted in
all to 200,370 acres. In March 1830 he purchased for
$30,000 certain tracts of Pennsylvania coal lands
which have to-day a fabulous value. But the land
which chiefly held his interest was those few acres of
his farm. "At my age the sole amusement which I enjoy is to be in the country constantly busy in attending to the work of the farm generally." The peace and
happiness of this final episode made a happy ending of
Girard's long, useful, and successful life.

"The accumulation of money interested him but little. He had now entered on his eighty-first year. His will was made and his great wealth dedicated to the good of posterity. He was under no incentive to labor for its increase. Yet in his bank, in his counting-house, on his farm, he continued to toil as of old from the sheer love of work."

At the time of his death in 1831, Girard had for fifty-five years been a resident of Philadelphia, and for practically his entire mature life a citizen of the United States. His funeral was of "immense extent"; the streets were thronged by people assembled to pay "a last tribute of respect to a great public benefactor."

The estate left by Girard amounted to almost seven million dollars, an amount which, in consideration of the times, would compare with the greatest fortunes of the present day. By the terms of his will, although there were many large charitable bequests, the bulk of the fortune was bequeathed to the city of Philadelphia, to be used in building and maintaining a school "to provide for such a number of poor male white orphan children . . . a better education as well as a more comfortable maintenance than they usually receive from the application of the public funds."

Certain other provisions have kept alive the memory of the testator's downrightness and individuality. In a paragraph of the will, Girard enjoined and required that "no ecclesiastic, missionary, or minister of any sect whatsoever shall ever hold or exercise any station or duty whatever in the said college, nor shall any such person ever be admitted for any purpose, or as a visitor, within the premises appropriated to the purposes of the said college. In making this restriction, I do not mean to cast any reflection upon any sect or person whatever; but as there is such a multitude of sects, and such diversity of opinion among them, I desire to keep the tender minds of the orphans, who are to derive advantage from this bequest, free from the excitements which clashing doctrines and sectarian controversy are apt to produce."

Under the wise management of the trustees of the estate, the public bequests of Girard can now be reckoned in millions. By the thrift, daring, and vision of a poor French sailor lad a great city of a mighty nation has received incalculable benefit throughout a century past, and will receive increasing benefit for centuries to come. Grasping eagerly the unlimited opportunities of the Republic where all men stand surefooted in the equal race for the highest rewards that civilization can bestow, he seized for himself the honors of high citizenship, the satisfaction of sincere philanthropy, and the pleasures that the possession of vast wealth profitably employed can bring.

To every boy of foreign birth the United States today holds equal promise. Not in mass movements, where progress is measured in the terms of the slowest, is the reward to be achieved. Only by effort honestly and sincerely given, in a land where opportunity is free to all, can the heights be reached. America, oldest of republics, cradle of liberty, extends its welcome to the youth that is and is to come, as its welcome has been extended to the youth of generations past.

II

JOHN ERICSSON

Born in Nordmark, Sweden, 1803
Died in New York City, 1889

HIGH up in the dark forests of Wermland, an ancient division of Sweden, where deep cold lakes feed the great rivers with clear water and send them down the mountains to the sea, was born, in the year 1803, a baby, John Ericsson, who in the years that followed made for himself a name which brought glory to the United States, the land of his adoption, and undying fame to the country of his birth.

There were few comforts or pleasures waiting to welcome young Ericsson into the world. The little village where he was born rested high in the mountains within six degrees of the Arctic Circle. All around were dark and gloomy forests, filled with strange legends and tales of ancient heroes, handed down from grandfather to father and from father to son. The hard thin soil of the mountains was unfit for cultivation, and it was difficult for the people of the forest villages to live on the poor crops which they produced in the few acres hewn from the forests.

But down beneath the tree-roots, deep-lying in the mountain-sides, were vast deposits of iron ore, renowned throughout the world as the material of the finest cutlery. So the deep iron-mines gave to the inhabitants of these mountain villages a hard-earned living which tempered their own spirits with that same quality which the Swedish iron developed in the blade of steel.

Olaf Ericsson, the father of John, was part owner of a small iron-mine and also superintendent of an iron-works, and so the small boy, with few playmates and none of the school advantages of the American lad of the present day, found his play and early education in the machinery at the mine and foundry. He was an industrious boy, and he was quick to discover the interest and inspiration of the things which surrounded him. All day, with pieces of paper, a pencil, and some drawing-tools which he had made for himself, he studied the principles of the machines and drew clear designs of them to illustrate their construction.

When John was eleven years old, his father left the mining village of Langbanshyttan and took with him his wife and his three children: John, Nils, a year older than John, and a sister, the oldest of the three. For many years the Swedish Government had considered the building of a great ship-canal which would open navigation across the Swedish peninsular, and it was as foreman of this project that Olaf Ericsson settled his family at Forsvik, a hundred miles from the old mountain home.

The mechanical features of this great engineering work filled young Ericsson with wonder and enthusiasm, and in his eagerness to obtain knowledge, in order that he too might participate, he sought information and education from everyone who had the time

J Ericsson

JOHN ERICSSON

19

and inclination to help him. From a boarder in his
father's household John learned to draw maps and
plans with skill and accuracy. A friendly professor
aided his architectural drawing, and one winter he
studied chemistry and learned to make his own inks
and colors with a few pennies' worth of chemicals
bought from the town druggist. In these years he also
learned the French language, Latin, and grammar; a
fine foundation which enabled him in after years to
express himself in speech and writing with a clearness
and exactness that proved of immeasurable assistance
to him.

At the age of twelve the boy had so progressed in
his studies that he was commissioned to make some
drawings for the canal company; and in the following
year he became assistant leveler, and a year later,
leveler. In this work he was required to make plans
and calculations for the canal, and had a monthly
salary, quarters, and traveling expenses. Undoubtedly John possessed unusual ability, but this extraor-
dinary promotion of so young a boy must in large
measure have been the result of his conscientious devotion to his studies and his enthusiasm and ambition
in his work.

In his leisure hours the boy found pleasure in building small working models of machinery, and among
these was a model of a saw-mill which many years
later he counted as the first in the long list of celebrated inventions which had brought him fame and
prosperity. This model was built entirely of wood,
with the exception of the band-saw, which was filed

out by hand from a broken watch-spring and was operated by a crank cast from an old tin spoon. A cord
served for the driving-band. No detail was omitted,
and when water was turned into the miniature water-
wheel, the machinery operated perfectly. With similar ingenuity he made for himself draughtsman's
compasses, from birchwood and broken needles; and
from the hairs in an old fur garment of his mother's
he laboriously fashioned brushes with which to apply
colors, also of his own making, to his drawings.

But now the father's health broke beneath the
weight of his work; the small earnings which supported the family dwindled, and each year that went
by gave to the growing boys added responsibilities.
In 1820 John realized that the time had come for him
to take his own path and begin actively to build for his
future. His father had died in the previous year and
his mother and sister were supporting themselves by
taking as boarders the workers on the canal. It was
necessary that he also should contribute to their
comfort.

Realizing the physical and moral value of military
training, young Ericsson joined the Swedish army.
He was now seventeen, a fine powerful fellow with
smooth active muscles, a clear eye, and a well-trained
brain. When he was eighteen there were few, if any,
of his fellows who could match him in feats of strength
or agility, and on one occasion he is said to have lifted
a cannon weighing over six hundred pounds.

Advancement came rapidly, and he was soon recognized as an expert artillery draughtsman and an

expert in the science of artillery, a branch of the service in which he had begun to specialize. It will be interesting to see how this early army experience gave to Ericsson knowledge which in later life brought him his greatest fame and enabled him to turn the tide of history and hold nations attentive before his words.

The stirring mind of the young man now yearned for a wider horizon than the Swedish army afforded, and for a greater opportunity than his own country presented. For several years he had been experimenting with a new type of engine by which he hoped to obtain greater horse-power with economy of fuel. England seemed to offer the opportunity, and in 1826 he left his native land and took up his residence in London.

Ericsson went to England at the opening of an engineering era. The employment of steam as a motive power was in its infancy. Travel by sea was entirely by ships; on land the stage-coach and canal-boat furnished the only means of transportation. The steam-engine was an undeveloped toy of science. Electricity in its industrial application was unknown.

Forming a business partnership with an English machine manufacturer, John Braithwaite, under the firm name of Ericsson and Braithwaite, Ericsson immediately turned his tremendous faculties to various engineering improvements and inventions. First a gas-engine occupied his interest; then he turned to his former conception of a "flame-engine," in which, by putting the actual fire directly under the piston, the expanding air would supply the motor power. In 1828 he built and put into operation in a tin-mine in Cornwall a water-pump driven by compressed air — an invention on which he later based his claim as inventor of a machine utilizing compressed air for transmitting power.

It was in the year 1819 that the Atlantic was for the first time crossed by a steam vessel, the United States ship Savannah, and this revolutionizing event stimulated Ericsson to new endeavors. In the months following he produced a number of important improvements by which smaller and lighter boilers were made possible by increasing the heat, and hence the power, of the fire by forced draught, as well as many other radical improvements in steam-engines and boiler-construction. Of these he claims particularly the credit of the invention of "surface condensation applied to steam navigation."

The first steam fire-engine — an apparatus which to-day constitutes perhaps the most important feature of a city's fire department — was invented and built by Ericsson in 1829. Previously, and as a matter of fact for years afterward, hand-operated engines, manned by crews of volunteer firemen, fought the fires which so frequently destroyed vast sections of the wood-constructed cities of those early days. It is not surprising that this valuable invention did not receive immediate recognition, for inventors rarely obtain such recognition from the people whom their inventions benefit. In fact, Ericsson's portable steam fire-engine was actually condemned as an impracticable contrivance that could serve no useful purpose.

To-day we travel thousands of miles by railroad; a hundred years ago our great-great-grandfathers traveled by horse-drawn coaches. Where we may now speed a mile a minute behind a giant steam locomotive, they were content with what seemed to them the tremendous speed of eleven miles an hour. But all things change. There are always leaders in the world's progress. Of these leaders was John Ericsson. Travel had been a luxury of the rich; the invention of the steam locomotive made fast and economical travel possible to the poor as well.

In 1829 a prize of two thousand five hundred dollars was offered for the best steam locomotive which could draw a weight of twenty tons at the rate of ten miles an hour. Ericsson had never built a locomotive, but he entered the contest. His greatest competitor was George Stephenson, who for several years had built small locomotives for use in coal mines.

On the great day of the trial thousands of people thronged the track to witness the novel sight. Never in the world's history had there been a public experiment so momentous, unless we except the journey of the American inventor's steamship, the Clermont, on her first historic progress up the Hudson River.

The locomotive entered in the contest by Stephenson was named the Rocket, a stong well-built engine that ultimately was awarded the prize. But although he was not the winner in this great competition, to Ericsson belongs great credit, for his locomotive, the Novelty, passed the Rocket at the amazing speed, for those days, of thirty miles an hour, and failed to win the prize only because of certain defects in its construction which caused it to break down before the goal was reached.

Ericsson was twenty-six years old when he built the Novelty. Already he had contributed many useful inventions to the world. But his greatest triumphs were still to come. He had been beaten fairly and squarely by Stephenson, but his was not the spirit that is easily subdued. Ericsson, like the hero of Greek mythology, rose the stronger each time an adversary cast him to the earth.

In 1836 he married a nineteen-year-old English girl, Amelia Byam, granddaughter of Sir Charles Byam, some time British Commissioner for Antigua.

For a short time he devoted himself to the perfection of a hot-air engine, and a sounding device by which ships might ascertain the depth of the water over which they were passing. Then he turned to a new activity. The result was revolutionary. What he had almost accomplished in the field of land-transportation with the Novelty, he now actually achieved in steam-navigation on the sea. To Ericsson should be credited the perfection and application of the screw for the propulsion of steam-driven vessels.

Up to the dawn of the nineteenth century the sailing-ship had ruled the seas. And even until the middle of that century the fast clippers, with their towers of widespread canvas, had held supreme domination over the world's waterways. But in the year 1835 Ericsson designed a rotary propeller driven by a steam-engine, which marked the beginning of the end of sailing days. The steam-engine, first placed in a ship by Robert Fulton, the American inventor, was no novelty, but it had been used only to propel vessels by means of paddle-wheels attached to each side of the vessels, huge cumbersome contrivances, which were easily damaged by heavy seas and which on ships of war afforded easy targets for the enemy.

The screw of Ericsson's was designed to operate underneath the stern of the vessel, under water and just forward of the rudder, exactly as it is placed to-day. To test this new invention Ericsson built a small vessel, the Francis B. Ogden, which was launched in the Thames River in the spring of 1837. The experiment was a great success and a speed of over ten miles an hour was attained, to the wonder of the stolid English boatmen who watched in amazement this strange ship move rapidly through the water with no visible means of propulsion.

Later in the summer Ericsson invited the Lords of the British Admiralty to inspect his steamship, and even conducted them on a trial trip on the Thames; but the amazing performance of the Ogden created but little interest in the minds of the British officials, who dismissed the affair as an "interesting experiment."

But Ericsson had a friend who stood him in good stead. This friend was an American, Francis B. Ogden, our counsul at Liverpool, after whom Ericsson's first vessel was named. Ogden was not an engineer, but he recognized in the Swedish inventor a man of sincerity and genius, and to his friendship Ericsson owed much in the way of advice and assistance.

In 1838 Ericsson built and launched a larger steamship, the Robert F. Stockton which sailed from
Gravesend, England, on April 13, 1839, and made a
successful passage to New York City, the first screw-
driven steamship ever to cross the Atlantic. As the
result of this remarkable achievement Ericsson was
assured that the government of the United States
would try out his invention on a large scale, and
persuaded him to go to America.

Ericsson was not reluctant. For years he had
struggled under the old-world conservatism. With his
energy and ambition, he realized that only in the great
land of opportunity beyond the sea could lie his hope
of recognition. In November, 1839, he sailed for the
United States.

There were no steam vessels in our navy when
Ericsson reached our shores, and it was not until 1842
that the building of the Princeton gave him the opportunity to display his great invention. The Princeton was a small iron warship of six hundred tons, and
to her construction Ericsson contributed not only his
screw-propeller, but also a new construction for the
gun-carriage, and, of even greater importance, a cannon reinforced by steel hoops shrunk on to the breech
of the gun. This reinforcing of the breech of a cannon
may be said to have established the recognized construction of the modern high-power naval guns of the
present day.

The Princeton marked a new advance in naval construction. Her speed, the location of her machinery below the water-line and hence out of danger

from an enemy's guns, her novel screw-propulsion, and her powerful armament made her the centre, not only of national, but of world interest.

For a number of years following, Ericsson continued his development of the science of naval engineering, and in 1843 applied for the first time twin-screw engines to the steamship Marmora. During these years recognition began to bring to the great inventor the financial rewards which he had long deserved. In the year 1844 his receipts from his inventions and contracts amounted to almost $40,000, and the following year he received almost $85,000. But the road to wealth and glory contains many obstacles, and the successes that crowned the work of these few years were in a large measure balanced by reverses, although in the end triumph out-balanced all.

For several years Ericsson devoted his energies to the perfection of a model type of warship, but his untiring efforts received scant recognition from the government. October 28, 1848, was, however, a day memorable, not only in the life of Ericsson, but in the history of the United States, for on that day he became a naturalized citizen. Born in a foreign land, a sojourner in European countries, it was but natural that the Swedish genius should find in this young nation of opportunity the field which he needed for the expression of his wonderful faculties. By his naturalization, Ericsson brought to the United States the fine inheritance of an ancient nation, and infused into the blood of the new republic additional strength and virility. Save for the native

Indian, there is no true American; but in the mingled blood of the people of many lands may be found to-day a race that combines the best of the nations of the earth, a composite people, free, prosperous, and masters of their own glorious destiny.

For many years Ericsson had held faith in the theory of a hot-air engine in which heated air would produce the effect of steam, but with greater economy. With characteristic confidence he carried his experiments to their completion, and expended practically his entire capital on the necessary models and machines which the working-out of his plans required. Success crowned his efforts, and the hot-air, or caloric, engine was generally conceded to be a success.

As the result of these experiments a number of New York capitalists supplied the necessary money to construct a large steamship, the paddle-wheels of which were operated by caloric engines designed by Ericsson. The vessel was named after the inventor and was a most novel and radical departure from any vessel up to that time designed. Her cost exceeded half a million dollars: an investment which showed the high esteem in which her designer was held. The Ericsson was launched in September, 1852, and made her trial trip on January 4, 1853. Never had so strong or fine a ship been built; the newspapers of the day were filled with praise, and her designer received from every quarter the most extravagant congratulations for the mechanical marvel which he had created.

But unexpected disaster destroyed in a few seconds the product of these months of thought and energy.

Within a few weeks of her launching the Ericsson encountered a tornado, and capsized and sank a few miles off New York Light. Although she was believed by many to mark the end of the use of steam-power and the beginning of a new era of hot-air dynamics, it is now recognized that this invention reached its maximum development in the Ericsson; and it is in connection with a later and far greater invention that history has accorded recognition to the designer's great mechanical genius.

Long before Ericsson left England he had thought out the plans for a strange kind of vessel, protected with iron, which would be able to fight and defeat any warship of any size. In 1854, the year in which he perfected the plan for his new type of warship, the navies of all the great nations were composed, in large part, of huge wooden vessels, usually sailing-ships, but a few combining sails and steam. For a number of years the use of iron-plating, or armor, on the sides of battleships had been discussed, and in 1845 R. L. Stevens, an American engineer, actually began the construction of a vessel, or "floating battery," encased in metal.

To France however, probably belongs the credit for the construction of the first ironclads, consisting of these floating batteries, the Lave, Devastation, and Tonnante, protected by 4.25-inch iron plates, which were used during the Crimean War. The following year France began the construction of four ironclad steam frigates, and England immediately followed, with the construction of a number of similar vessels.

But the warship of John Ericsson in no way resembled the huge ironclads of France or England. With characteristic disregard for precedent he designed a ship which rested so low in the water that only about three feet of its sides would be exposed. The sides and deck were protected by heavy plates of iron, and in the centre of the deck was a circular heavily armored turret which revolved in either direction and contained powerful guns. These vessels, or monitors, as Ericsson named them, were to be propelled by steam. The particular advantages of the type were that so little of the craft showed above the water that it afforded an exceedingly small target to an enemy; that the heavy plating protected it from hostile shot, and the revolving target enabled the crew to fire in any direction without manœuvring the vessel, while such shot as might strike the turret would glance harmlessly from its circular side.

During the Crimean War Ericsson offered the plans for this remarkable vessel to the French Emperor; but they were politely declined as impractical in much the same way in which, some years earlier, the British Admiralty had declined to consider the screw-propeller as little more than an amusing experiment.

When war was declared in 1861 between the Northern States and the Confederate States of the South, Ericsson was fifty-eight years old. In this national calamity in which brother was armed against brother, and the fate of the country seemed hanging by a thread, Ericsson unhesitatingly cast himself with those who sought the preservation of the Union and the abolition of slavery from the United States. Never before had his adopted country needed so vitally his tremendous services. With superb health derived from a normal life of conservative habits, and a brain trained by long years of engineering experiment, Ericsson found himself ready and able to meet the call for his greatest service to the nation.

The United States navy at the beginning of the war was composed entirely of wooden vessels. Early in 1861 the Confederates began the construction of a floating battery heavily armored with iron. For this purpose the old United States frigate Merrimac, which had been burned and sunk in the Norfolk Navy Yard, was raised, and the work of encasing her with armor plates was begun.

Meanwhile, in the North, Congress had called for proposals for ironclad steam vessels, and less than a month later, Ericsson addressed to President Lincoln a letter in which he offered to submit the plans of a monitor, and described the advantages of its unique design. On September 13, Ericsson went to Washington and personally laid before the Navy Department his plans and received a contract to proceed with the construction of the Monitor.

The keel was laid on October 25, and on January 30, she slid down the ways into the water. A month later she was commissioned. The Monitor was 172 feet in length and displaced 776 tons. In the centre of her low flat deck was the revolving turret, twenty feet in diameter, protected by eight inches of iron-plating. Two heavy guns were mounted in the turret. The vessel was operated entirely by steam-engines, placed well below the water-line, which propelled a screw beneath the overhanging stern.

Rushed to completion in the brief period of three months, the Monitor was barely commissioned in time to render, at Hampton Roads, the tremendous service which in a few brief hours revolutionized naval warfare, made obsolete the navies of the world, rescued the Union navy from crushing disaster, and immortalized the name of John Ericsson, her designer and constructor.

The Monitor had been intended to serve with Admiral Farragut's fleet at New Orleans, but a crisis nearer at hand made a sudden change of plans necessary. The Monitor left New York on the afternoon of March 6, 1862, under command of Lieutenant John L. Worden, U.S.N., and arrived at Hampton Roads on the evening of March 8, after a stormy passage.

Meanwhile the armored Confederate ram Merrimac had created havoc with the great wooden warships of the Federal navy. On the seventh, the Merrimac had rammed and sunk the frigate Cumberland, and then destroyed the Congress, vessels powerless to inflict injury on the iron sides of the Confederate ram. The tall frigates, St. Lawrence, Roanoke, and Minnesota, powerless to resist or to escape, awaited their inevitable destruction on the following day.

But on that eventful morning, as the Merrimac steamed out into the stream to complete her work, which would break the blockade the Federal forces had established, the Monitor glided out from under the stern of the Minnesota, looking for all the world like "a barrel-head afloat with a cheese-box on top of it."

For four hours these two strange vessels fought this greatest duel of naval history, which, on the ships and the shores, was watched by the anxious eyes of soldiers and sailors of North and South to whom the outcome was of such tremendous import. Manœuvring like boxers, the two vessels circled each other, black smoke pouring from their low funnels and the red flame of the great guns spurting from the gun-ports. As she had rammed the Cumberland, so did the Merrimac endeavor to crush the Monitor with her ram; but the Monitor either slipped past her heavier and more ungainly adversary or allowed the Merrimac to push her aside. Round and round the circular turret swung, turning away in order to load the two guns which protruded, and then swinging back to deliver a volley of metal against the plated sloping side of the Merrimac.

Unable to damage the Monitor and herself severely pounded by the forty-one shots which the Monitor had fired, the Merrimac finally withdrew, leaving the strange warship of the Swedish-American inventor the victor. The Minnesota, the Roanoke, and the St. Lawrence were saved. The blockade remained unbroken.

In the words of a Confederate who witnessed the battle, "The Monitor was by immense odds the most formidable vessel of war on this planet."

During the following years of the war, Ericsson

4

devoted his vast energies to the service of his country, and at great financial loss and immeasurable personal sacrifice constructed a large number of vessels of the Monitor type for the navy.

With the close of the war Ericsson continued the marvelous series of inventions which he had given to the world. For a number of years he gave his best thought to the building and mounting of heavy guns; and later he turned his energies to the construction of a practical submarine torpedo. In these later experiments he personally invested over a hundred thousand dollars.

From the United States and foreign countries came recognition of his services to the world. In 1866 the Department of State offered him the appointment of Commissioner to the Universal Exposition at Paris. The previous year he had received a resolution of thanks from the Swedish Parliament. Among other honors conferred upon him were his election to the Franklin Institute of Philadelphia, honorary memberships in the Royal Military Academy of Science of Stockholm and the Royal Military Academy of Sweden, a joint resolution of thanks from the United States Congress, a resolution from the State of New York, the Rumford gold and silver medals, and a gold medal from the Society of Iron Masters of Sweden. In 1863 he received the honorary degree of LL.D. from Wesleyan University; and later he was made a Knight Commander with the Grand Cross of the order of the North Star and a Commander of St. Olaf, two Swedish honors. In later years came many other distinctions, not only from the United States and Sweden, but from Denmark, Spain, and Austria.

In these later years came also many demands on Ericsson's generosity, and to the near members of his family, and even to his most distant relatives, he invariably responded with a substantial gift. Realizing the tremendous value of education, he gave freely when money was needed to provide schooling for the children of members of his family whom he had never seen. But these benefactions to relatives and friends were invariably made only when Ericsson believed in the true need and the sincerity of the request. Out of the considerable income which came to him from his inventions in later years he gave also with a liberal hand whenever public or private distress was brought to his attention.

Ericsson's own wants were few. His temperate habits, his love of physical exercise, and his simple tastes made but slender demands on his income. Vigorous by inheritance, and possessing a fine physique from his early activities, he preserved his splendid vigor throughout his long life. Rarely has been given to the world a finer example of health and character contributing to a career of splendid usefulness.

On the eighth of March, 1889, John Ericsson died in his New York house, where for a quarter of a century he had lived his active and solitary existence. The significance of his death was recognized, not only by his native Sweden and the United States, the land of his adoption, but by the entire civilized world, in which his inventions had brought such revolutionizing changes. But the story of his achievements can never die, and in the history of his useful life is an inspiration to every succeeding generation to whom the United States unfolds an ever-increasing opportunity.

III

LOUIS AGASSIZ

Born in Motier, Switzerland, 1807
Died in Cambridge, Massachusetts, 1873

WHEN men first received the names which they have handed down through succeeding generations there was undoubtedly an appropriate reason for the name which each man bore. The Smiths quite probably worked with iron, the Carpenters labored with saw and hammer, and the son of John became Johnson to his friends. But centuries have passed, and it rarely happens to-day that a man's name describes his vocation or his characteristics.

Occasionally, however, there is an exception, and the name of Agassiz is one of these. Lover of nature, and particularly of the living things which have for hundreds of thousands of years inhabited the earth, Louis Agassiz bore a name that suggested his ruling interests; for Agassiz, or Aigasse as it was written in old French, is the name of the magpie, a lovable, friendly bird that was known to every peasant in the beautiful countryside of La Sarraz.

Louis Agassiz was a naturalist and a geologist. Wise in all departments of these wide fields of nature study, and the leading teacher in his time, he will always be remembered for his discoveries in two particular departments of his great subject. Agassiz was an ichthyologist and a palæontologist. These are hard Latin names, but they are easily understood, for an ichthyologist is a man who studies fishes, and a palæontologist is one who is a student of the ancient life of the globe as it may be seen in the fossil remains deep buried in the earth. Moreover, to the science of geology Agassiz contributed a great discovery which revolutionized the thought of scientists of his day; for it was he who proved beyond all doubt that at one time, far back in the world's history, great moving glaciers covered a huge part of the earth's surface, and where now the summer sunshine warms green fields, at one time, in an arctic temperature, these same lands were deep buried under grinding, creeping fields of ice.

Not far from Lake Neuchâtel, in western Switzerland, is the little village of Motier, a place so small that it is hard to find it on the maps of ordinary atlases. Below the village the blue water of Lake Morat gleams like a bit of sky in the green of hills and fields, and beyond, like a blue wall against the sky, the Bernese Alps look down over the ancient country.

Here on May 28, 1807, was born Jean Louis Rudolph Agassiz. His father was a clergyman and his mother the daughter of a physician, and the boy inherited from them a love of study and a delight in teaching which always distinguished him. From the beautiful country of his birth came also an inheritance of nature that kept him throughout his long life always a boy at heart.

The lakes of Switzerland are among the oldest dwelling-places of mankind since human life began.

Beneath the waters of Lake Morat are still found traces of an ancient race that once lived there in huts built over the water; still may be seen, far down in the blue deeps, the earthen vessels which, perhaps, fell from their dwellings; occasionally are found the stumps of piles on which their houses rested. They were a water-loving people, and Agassiz, born on the shores of the same lake as this ancient people, found in the water a natural and congenial element.

He was a normal, wholesome boy, but from the very first his love of nature displayed itself at every turn. He delighted in birds and animals and insects, and he was constantly scouring the vineyard-clad hillsides and the woods and meadows for new specimens. But it was on the waters of the lakes and in their cold clear depths that his insatiate curiosity found its greatest gratification. He was a skilful fisherman and he soon learned the haunts and habits of every kind of fish that dwelt there. With his brother Auguste, the bright summer days fled past in one long excursion. Like the fish which they hunted, the boys found in the lakes a friendly element. They were splendid swimmers, so skilled that they would often abandon entirely the hook and line, and, diving swiftly into the water, catch the gliding fish in their hands.

Like all boys who live in the country, Louis had made collections of every kind, and in the garden near the house he kept constantly increasing families of rabbits, field-mice, guinea-pigs, and birds. These were not merely pets which he loved and cared for; even in his youthful eyes they seemed to have a deeper significance, for he studied them and observed their habits in a way that gave him a basis for the scientific observations of his later life.

It was natural that such a boy should be fearless, and in this respect Louis was far above the average. Strong, alert, and resourceful, he was a splendid swimmer and a strong skater. Many are the tales of boyish fearlessness that are told about him, tales of boating exploits, of long excursions, and particularly of how once he made a bridge of his body across a deep fissure in the ice too wide to jump, that his brother Auguste might creep across.

When he was ten years old, his active schooling began. In the nearby town of Bienne was a public school for boys. The rules were strict and the hours long, for the boys were required to study for nine hours every day. But the father had given Louis a good grounding in the elements of education, and this, combined with his natural aptitude, gave him an advantage over his fellow students.

Vacations, however, were as welcome to Louis and his brother as they are to boys of the present day; and long before dawn on the first day of each vacation, the two boys would be up and homeward bound, swinging along the twenty miles of country road which lay between Bienne and Motier. These were happy days, for although the Agassiz family had but the very small income which the office of a country minister afforded, there was a wealth of good fun and love and wholesome out-of-door happiness in the lives of the young people who made merry in the little town.

Four years were spent at the school at Bienne, and as the end of the fourth year neared, Louis, although only fourteen years old, announced to his parents his desire to become an author. "I wish to advance in the sciences," he wrote his father. "I have resolved to become a man of letters." And then he expressed his hope that he might be permitted, after spending a year and a half in commerce at Neuchatel, to pass four years at a university in Germany, and finally finish his studies at Paris. "Then, at the age of twenty-five," he concluded, "I could begin to write." Mature ambitions these, for a boy of fourteen years!

It was fortunate that the elder Agassiz recognized in the boy those qualities which were uppermost, and encouraged his studious desires. The year and a half of business training was abandoned, and in its place Louis was sent for two years of additional study at the College of Lausanne. Already he had felt the charm of study, and his boyish pastimes had now become studious investigations which absorbed his interest and energy. His work was as orderly as his mind; his notebooks, written with remarkable neatness in a small fine handwriting, are excellent examples of clear classification of whatever branch of study he undertook. Everything was arranged and classified; subjects were clearly separated and subdivided under marked headings; nothing was begun that was not completed in every detail.

At Lausanne, Agassiz had access to the first natural history collection that he had ever seen; and there also he found friends who sympathized with his favorite tastes. While he was at Lausanne, it was decided that he should study medicine, a profession which would meet his natural inclinations and at the same time ultimately yield him the income necessary for his support.

Accordingly, during his seventeenth year, Louis entered the medical school at Zürich. Here he found still more congenial surroundings; for among the faculty of the university were men of reputation in the particular branches of natural history which most deeply interested him. Under the professor of natural history the study of ornithology was opened to him. Here also the sciences of zoölogy and geology were taught, and Louis eagerly enrolled in the classes that were held in these subjects.

In 1826, after two years at Zürich, Louis entered the great German University of Heidelberg, and there his true university life began. The four years that he passed there were among the most important years of his entire life. They were years of hard conscientious study, combined with wholesome recreation. "First at work, and first at play," was his motto. Here he made friendships that were tense and enduring. Two fellow students, Braun and Schimper, became particularly his intimates, and with Agassiz formed a trio which their fellow students called "the Little Academy."

It was an ambitious atmosphere, and the friendships which were formed were based on a love of intellectual pleasures. There was also the vivid vital student life beyond the classrooms; there were long excursions on foot in vacation times; there were duels and love-affairs, and there were boisterous evenings thick with tobacco smoke. Agassiz was a powerful gymnast and an expert fencer. There was nothing in the student life that was good in which he did not participate.

Of the many friendships which his open and affectionate nature so easily formed, his friendship with Alexander Braun was deepest and most lasting. Soon he began to visit Braun at his home in Carlsruhe, where he met his friend's two talented sisters, one of whom was later to become his wife. And it was here, in the spring of 1827, that the friendly Braun family nursed him back to health after a serious attack of typhoid fever.

The earnestness of these young men is perhaps best described by Agassiz himself. "When our lectures are over, we meet in the evening at Braun's room or mine, with three or four intimate acquaintances, and talk of scientific matters, each one in his turn presenting a subject which is first developed by him and then discussed by all. These exercises are very instructive. As my share, I have begun to give a course of natural history, or rather of pure zoölogy. Braun talks to us of botany; and another of our company, Mahir, teaches us mathematics and physics in his turn; Schimper will be our professor of philosophy. Thus we shall form a little university, instructing one another, and at the same time learning what we teach more thoroughly, because we shall be obliged to demonstrate it."

From Heidelberg the three companions now transferred their studies to the new University of Munich, where a far more stimulating intellectual life awaited them. Here were some of the most celebrated teachers of the day, and "the city teemed with resources for the student in arts, letters, philosophy, and science." A fine spirit existed between students and professors, and there was constant opportunity, not only in the classrooms, but beyond their walls, for the earnest young men to draw on the wells of information which their brilliant instructors freely afforded them.

With an allowance of only $250 a year, Agassiz's life was necessarily simple and severe. But the three companions soon found that their humble rooms had become the meeting-place of the most brilliant men in the University. Students and even professors crowded their simple living quarters, and naturalists of renown came to visit these extraordinary young men. "Someone was always coming or going; the half-dozen chairs were covered with books, piled one upon another — the bed, also, was used as a seat, and as a receptacle for specimens, drawings and papers." Specimens of various sorts decorated the walls. In Agassiz's own room were several hundred fish, "shut up in a wooden tub with a cover and in various big glass jars. A live gudgeon with beautiful stripes is wriggling in his wash-bowl, and he has adorned his table with monkeys."

During their vacations the young men made expeditions to see such museums as were within reach, and to visit any scientific men to whom they could obtain an introduction. All of southern Germany was included in their rambles, and their wanderings carried them even into explorations of extensive tracts of the Alps.

But although Agassiz had come to Munich for the special purpose of taking the degree of doctor of medicine, his studies soon drifted from those of a medical student to the studies of a true naturalist. He had gone to Heidelberg "with a strong taste for natural history; he left Munich devoted heart and soul to science." Under these circumstances it was only natural that his first degree should be that of doctor of philosophy; but a year later, to fulfill the desires of his parents, he received the degree of doctor of medicine and surgery.

Up to this time Agassiz had paid no particular attention to the study of ichthyology, which was later to become the great occupation of his life; but in 1829 he was unexpectedly given the opportunity to prepare a history of the fresh-water fishes of Brazil, from a collection which had been made by a celebrated scientist who had died before he could prepare the report covering the collection. Agassiz threw himself enthusiastically into the work of describing and figuring these Brazilian fishes, and in 1829 the work was completed and published with the name of the youthful author on the title-page. His life-work was begun.

It was at this time that he wrote to his father: "I wish it may be said of Louis Agassiz that he was the first naturalist of his time, a good citizen, and a good son, beloved by those who know him."

In the autumn of 1830 Agassiz left Munich, and

after a short visit in Vienna, where he found himself "received as a scientific man for whom no letters of recommendation were necessary," he returned to Switzerland and the welcome of his proud parents. But it was hard to adjust himself to the quiet village by Lake Morat, and, although money was difficult to secure, a visit to Paris was finally made possible through the generosity of a friend of the family. Here Agassiz formed important friendships with two of the greatest scientists of the age: Cuvier, the leading French zoölogist, and Alexander von Humboldt, the leader of the scientific world.

The years that immediately followed were filled with scientific progress. The " Brazilian Fishes " had determined Agassiz's specialty, and the reputation of the book led him to plan a history of the fresh-water fishes of Central Europe, including a natural history of fossil fishes. It was an enormous undertaking, for palæontology was a new science, involving the study of fossil specimens scattered through the museums of Europe. But Agassiz foresaw only the value which science would place on such a work, and the five volumes were finally published by him, at intervals, from 1833 to 1843.

Life in Paris soon proved difficult for the young scientist, and his poverty was particularly noticeable, for here there was wealth and position even among scientific men. He had only forty dollars a month, and his clothing had become so worn that it was not possible for him to accept invitations from well-to-do friends. The position of professor of natural history at Neuchâtel was offered him, and, although the salary was only $400 a year, it seemed wise to accept. His acceptance, and with it the close of his year in Paris, marks the end of his boyhood and student days. A new period awaited him.

The college of Neuchâtel was small and unimportant. The chair of natural history was new, and there was no scientific apparatus, museum, or lecture-room. But this mattered little to the young professor. Soon after his arrival he founded a Natural History Society among the leading citizens of the town; his lectures were given in the city hall, and his own collection formed the nucleus of a natural history museum.

As in college, so in the quiet Swiss village, Agassiz soon gathered about him a group of scientific men as his students and assistants, many of whom in later life became themselves naturalists of reputation. It was a "scientific factory" of which Agassiz was the mainspring. He was poor, but somehow he managed to go on, supporting many of his staff in his own house, printing and lithographing his own publications, and supporting his own family as well, for his marriage had now brought additional responsibilities upon his broad shoulders. It was an unstable basis, but in one way or another Agassiz found the means to proceed. Money was but the means to an end, never the end itself. "I cannot spend my time in making money!" he once said when a profitable business offer was made to him. The remark expressed clearly his firm devotion to his chosen profession.

It was during this period of his life that Agassiz added to scientific knowledge the proof that at some remote time in the earth's existence vast glaciers, moving fields of ice miles in area and often hundreds of feet in thickness, had played a part in the earth's formation almost as important as the recognized agents, fire and water. It was a geological discovery the proof of which, although indisputable, seemed so startling, that it was with difficulty that it was accepted even by the best scientific minds of the day.

In the Alpine country had been found great boulders dropped apparently by some strange force in fields far from the quarries of native rock from which they had been torn. Here also were moraines and dikes, great piles of loose gravel deposited by some unknown agency; and here also, where the bedrock was visible, could be seen deep furrows and scratches on the polished stone as if chiseled by a giant tool.

Glaciers existed in the Alps, but it was hard for men to believe that glaciers had once existed where now were green fields and meadows. But Agassiz was not the man to endeavor to found a belief on unsupported theory, and only after six years of study of the glaciers and glacial traces in the Alps and actual observations on the glacier of the Aar, was he prepared to give his proofs of the theory to the scientific world.

Basing his demonstration on this accumulated evidence, Agassiz proved that at one time glaciers had covered a large part of the now civilized world. The great boulders had been scooped up by them in their progress, and perhaps some thousands of years later had been dropped a hundred miles away by the melting ice-sheet. So also had the masses of gravel been carried far from their sources, to form strange new glacial deposits. And on the scarred and grooved rocks was the final evidence; for these deep scratches had surely been ground by the advancing glacier as it slowly and silently moved onward. "The idea that such phenomena were not restricted to regions where glaciers now are found, but that traces of glacial action could be seen over enormous tracts of the earth's surface, perhaps including regions in the tropics, and that in countries now temperate there might be discovered, not only the remains of tropical fauna and flora, but also distinct indications of a period of arctic cold — this was as new as startling."

During the years of his professorship at Neuchâtel, Agassiz published many important contributions to scientific knowledge in those particular departments of natural science to which he had devoted himself. At the same time came also many honors, including offers of professorships from the universities of Geneva and Lausanne, and the award of the Wollaston Medal by the Geographical Society of London.

But the second period in Agassiz's life was drawing to a close: a great country beyond the Atlantic would soon be ready to receive him. Agassiz, the student and now the discoverer, was about to begin his final great activity as the pioneer and teacher of natural history to a strange people in a foreign land. Each year at Neuchâtel had plunged Agassiz deeper and deeper into debt; his situation had passed

5

from bad to well-nigh hopeless. Then, unexpectedly, help was offered. The King of Prussia offered him three thousand dollars, to be spent in travel for scientific purposes; and at the same time came an invitation from the Lowell Institute of Boston to visit the United States. Agassiz could not refuse. It was a solution of all his immediate difficulties; a wide horizon in the eager young republic spread before him. In September, 1846, Agassiz sailed for Boston.

He had left behind him all that is wealth to a scientific man. Books and collections were the tools of his trade; in his fellow naturalists he had found help and inspiration. In the United States bountiful nature had provided a fertile and unexplored field, but here he must work alone. "He came, perhaps, in a spirit of adventure and of curiosity; but he stayed because he loved a country where new things could be built up; where he could think and speak as he pleased; and where his ceaseless activity would be considered of high quality."

On his arrival in Boston Agassiz was cordially received by John A. Lowell, who, as trustee of the Lowell Institute, had extended to him the invitation which was in a large measure responsible for his coming. The course of lectures which Agassiz had planned for the Lowell Institute was entitled "The Plan of Creation." His success was immediate. The people were eager to hear the message of the great lecturer. A second course, on "Glaciers," was soon arranged, and in a few months Agassiz found himself the most popular lecturer in all the great Eastern cities.

The subjects which he chose were always of a character which made it possible for large untrained audiences to follow him and clearly understand the points which he logically developed. His command of English was at first faulty, but he was never embarrassed, and his audiences found a peculiar charm in his foreign accent and the unusual phrases which he so frequently employed. But the blackboard was his unfailing assistant, and as he talked, his quick hand illustrated the subject with sketches so simple and so clear that the lecture could almost have been comprehended by these alone.

He had left his collections behind him, but almost immediately new collections began to grow, and a new "scientific factory" was established in his house in East Boston. He always spoke of his specimens as "material for investigation," for to Agassiz every stone and every insect held a story filled with wonder and romance which only patient study could unfold. His house, his garden, and even his pockets were filled with "material"; as an illustration may be mentioned the occasion when Agassiz, on being asked by a lady sitting beside him at a dinner-party to explain the difference between a toad and a frog, instantly produced, to the amazement of his companions, a live frog and a live toad from his pockets.

It was but natural that Agassiz should find in Harvard University, the oldest and most celebrated seat of learning in the United States, the congenial atmosphere which his work required. And it is equally natural that the great University should recognize in

Agassiz a master-teacher who would prove a most desirable addition to its faculty. Agassiz had already found in the United States a cordial welcome and a deep appreciation. The year 1848 marks definitely the beginning of the last phase of his life, for in this year the death of his wife in Carlsruhe and his acceptance of the chair of zoölogy and geology at Harvard led him to abandon forever his thought of some day returning to his native land.

Two years later his marriage to Elizabeth Cabot Cary of Boston bound him still closer to the land of his adoption, and the remaining years of his life were years of consistent activity filled with growth and honor. An expedition to Lake Superior in 1848 was followed by a trip to study the Florida reefs in 1850 and a visit to the Mississippi River in 1853. During these years his collections were rapidly increased, and already he was planning for the establishment at Harvard of a great Museum of Natural History.

Life in Boston and in the clear atmosphere of the University must have been highly stimulating to a man of Agassiz's sensitive susceptibilities. Emerson, Holmes, Hawthorne, Motley, and Longfellow were his companions, and a group of brilliant younger minds surrounded him in his work.

From abroad now came honors the larger part of which Agassiz saw fit to decline. In 1852 the Prix Cuvier was awarded to him in recognition of his work on fossil fishes. A call to the University of Zürich was declined in 1854; and during the four years between 1857 and 1861 he three times declined a call to the chair of palæontology at Paris, perhaps the highest scientific honor which the world could afford. But neither honors nor wealth could tempt him. His affection for America and his love for his work in that appreciative country held him fast. In 1861 he became a naturalized citizen of the United States.

Rarely, if ever, was there a man of more lovable and winning personality. "Everybody sought his society, and no one could stand before his words and his smile. The fishermen at Nahant would pull two or three miles to get him a rare fish." Rich and poor, the educated and the uneducated, all paid homage to his magnetic personality. Physically large, his genial countenance and smiling eyes made friends with everyone. And at the same time those laughing brown eyes, that seemed made only for pleasure and jollity, "saw more than did all our eyes put together; for he looked, but we only stared."

The cornerstone of the great Museum of Comparative Zoölogy at Harvard was laid in 1859, and in the years that have followed, the collection has grown to proportions which make it a worthy memorial to its celebrated founder. Into this edifice Agassiz freely poured the material which he had collected on his many expeditions, including a wealth of specimens gathered in 1865 and 1866, on an expedition to Brazil; and in 1871 and 1872, in a specially designed ship, the Hassler, he rounded the Horn, and with dredging apparatus collected along both coasts of the South American continent valuable data concerning the fauna and physical conditions which were found at great depths. Meanwhile, although constantly neglectful of his own income, he devoted his rare personal persuasion to the cause of obtaining the large sum necessary for the building and maintenance of the Museum. And it is to him alone that credit is due for the money that was thus raised, at a cost to science of priceless hours of his own all-too-limited time and energy.

The intellect of Agassiz was gigantic, and yet he combined with his mighty forces an unfailing patience with dull or ignorant people. His craving for knowledge was equaled only by his ability in imparting it to others. Nothing that he achieved was for himself: his all was attained that he might give it to the world. "Good teachers are not commonly original investigators; and original investigators often lack both the will and power to tell other people what they know." To this Agassiz was perhaps the greatest exception that the world has ever seen. The scientific world will ever remember Louis Agassiz for his discoveries in zoölogy, for his vast researches in the study of fishes, and for his glacial theories and subsequent revelations in geology; but the world at large will hold him perhaps more dear as the master who brought to the United States the old sciences of an older civilization and, infusing them with his own vitality, became to the people of America the first and the great teacher of the history of the mighty book of nature, which before his time had remained closed to them.

On December 14, 1873, Louis Agassiz died at Cambridge, in the shadow of the walls of the great University of which he had become so loyal a member. Above his grave a simple granite boulder from the glacier of the Aar, sent by loving friends in the land of his birth, gives in its brief inscription the name of a man whom the United States proudly claims as citizen, and whom the world honors as a man.

IV

CARL SCHURZ

Born in Liblar, Germany, 1829
Died in New York City, 1906

THERE are few Americans who can say that they were born in a castle, for the castle-born children of Europe of whom history tells us have been the children of royalty who have by virtue of their birth inherited the privileges of a ruling clan and have ever handed down these same privileges to succeeding generations. Europe was for centuries ruled by the castle-born. Supreme was the tradition of royalty. And strange in contrast is the story of a baby of humble parentage who by chance first saw the light through the high windows of a castle wall, and lived to become an honored citizen of a land where royalty is unknown and all men are equal.

In the great republic of the United States, men who had become wearied of the old order of things had built a nation on another plan. Here there was no royalty; it was not where or how a boy was born that counted, but what kind of a man he became. To all, equal opportunities were offered. It was not who you were, but what you were, that counted; and that is what counts to-day in the United States.

The first President, George Washington, was a farmer. Abraham Lincoln was born in a log-cabin

C. Schurz.

and taught himself to read and write in the early days of his hard boyhood. Woodrow Wilson was a schoolteacher. Rich men and poor men have risen to the presidency; men with the blood of many nations in their veins. The log-cabin or the castle birthplace has counted little; high posts of honor have been won by all.

Carl Schurz was born in a castle at Liblar, a small German town a few miles distant from the great city of Cologne, in the year 1829. But in spite of his castle birthplace, Carl was not of royal blood, but a poor boy. Like the fathers of so many other distinguished sons, the elder Schurz was a schoolmaster; but so small was his pay that he and his family came to live with his wife's father, a tenant farmer, in the ancient castle at Liblar. And in this castle was born the boy Carl who, in the many years of his useful life, was destined to fill high places in the great Republic beyond the seas.

Life in the great castle was much the same in 1829 that it had been for hundreds of years, for changes came slowly in the peaceful, beautiful German country. At harvest-time the young and old, with a spirit of mutual helpfulness, gathered the harvest; and at other times they met for Rhineland festivals, with much happy visiting of relatives, with games and contests of strength and skill. In the big stone hall of the castle the "folk" assembled for their meals at long wooden tables, and ate their soup or porridge out of deep wooden bowls with wooden spoons. During the day the women spun flax at their spinning-wheels and the men worked in the shops, the stables, and the fields.

In the twilight hours the boy listened to stories of the "French Times," when the great Napoleon passed through the land with his mighty army before the Russian campaign, and later returned, his army shattered and defeated. He heard of the Cossacks, uncouth, dirty, bearded men on shaggy ponies, who followed Napoleon's retreating army, and how they stole and plundered and ate the tallow candles in people's houses. And he heard, too, of the great men whose fame was not created by the sword — Schiller, Goethe Tasso, Shakespeare, Voltaire, Rousseau. Perhaps the stories of these famous men of history inspired the boy in later years to become himself a leader among men.

When he was still very young, Carl was sent to school; and twice a week he walked, each way, to a town four miles distant, to study music. It was during these early days that Carl first heard his family talk about the United States, "that young Republic where the people were free, without kings, without counts"; and it is probable that the impressions of this republican state of free citizens received in his early years had something to do with the directing of his ambitions in later life.

When Carl was nine years old his father, believing that the boy had outgrown the little school at Liblar, sent him to a school at Brühl, where he continued his various lessons and the study of music. The next year Carl was taken by his father to Cologne and entered the "gymnasium," a school which bears some resemblance to the high school in the United States. Here he studied history, Latin, and German, and particularly the art of expressing himself in writing with clearness and ease — a study which perhaps contributed most to his success in coming years.

But now a new influence began to enter the life of the boy. During the first fifty years of the nineteenth century, that part of Germany which extends along the banks of the Rhine had seen three governments. First, it had been ruled by the Archbishop Electors; then it was conquered by the French and had felt French rule both under the French Republic and the Empire; and last of all, it had been taken from the French and annexed by Prussia. The Rhenish people perhaps liked the Prussian rule least of all; for the Prussians governed well, but with a stern discipline that could never be understood by the careless, pleasure-loving people of the Rhine.

Among the younger people, and particularly those of the better-educated class, among whom Carl found himself, there was a restless spirit and the feeling that great changes were necessary. Young men believed that the hard Prussian rule must be overthrown and give place to a new form of constitutional government, with free speech, free press, and free political institutions. How this was to be done, no one knew; but Carl and his companions talked much with each other of their dreams of liberty and unity for the Fatherland, and eagerly read every newspaper and pamphlet that fell into their hands, to keep themselves informed of the tendencies of the day.

It was the ambition of the elder Schurz that his son, after graduation from the gymnasium, should enter the famous university at Bonn. But only a year before Carl's graduation the father met with financial disaster which swept away the small savings of years and left him practically penniless. Carl was seventeen years old and was entering his last year in the gymnasium; by this disaster all his hopes and ambitions seemed swept aside. His father, bankrupt, was in a debtor's prison. Hurriedly, Carl took leave of his teachers and friends and returned home, where, by much hard effort, he succeeded in securing his father's release.

The question now arose whether or not he must abandon his studies and take up a new course of life. Next to his family, his ambition for a literary career was the greatest factor in his life. By leaving the gymnasium his hopes seemed destroyed beyond remedy; for the examinations for the university were very difficult and practically required this final year of study and preparation. Fortunately, his father in a few months became able again to provide for himself, and Carl immediately undertook the difficult task of preparing to pass the graduation examinations at Cologne, which must be accomplished before he could enter the university. By hard work this was finally accomplished, and Carl entered the university at Bonn.

German universities have always been known for their student societies. Too many of these groups of students have had a reputation only for drinking and senseless dueling; but there are others that have been marked by a distinct scientific, literary, or musical tone. Of the latter class was the Buschenschaft Franconia at Bonn; its members were not men of wealth or noble birth, but in later years they found high places in the world's history. And of this society Carl Schurz was elected a member. It was a group of young men who were destined greatly to affect his entire life.

But of even greater importance in their effect on the life of Carl Schurz were certain political conditions in Germany. Early in the century, after Napoleon's ill-fated campaign into Russia, the King of Prussia and the Russian Tsar had called the German people to arms, promising them a new national union, free political institutions, and the abolition of arbitrary government. The victories of Leipzig and Waterloo broke the power of Napoleon, but the years that followed did not see the promises of the Prussian King fulfilled. In 1814 the Congress of Vienna created an alliance among the German States, but the organization was composed of kings and princes; there was no popular representation and no mention of civic rights, a popular vote, a free press, freedom of assembly, or trial by jury — all of which were rights desired by the people.

Then followed a bitter period of studied repression of every liberal tendency, and the advance toward liberal institutions almost ceased. In 1840, Frederick William IV ascended the Prussian throne. It was at first believed that he sympathized with the liberal and patriotic hopes of the people; but it soon became evident that the same policy would be continued; the demands of the people were refused, and the press censorship was increased. Discontent with general conditions, and particularly with absolute kingly power and police despotism, soon became general, and in 1847 the King convoked a "United Diet" in Berlin, to consist of members of all the provincial diets. But only in appearance was this a popular assembly, and no reforms were, or could be, enacted by it.

Disappointment and discontent followed, and from the mass of people revolutionary agitators arose, demanding liberation from the rule of a domineering King. "God, Liberty, Fatherland" was the motto of the people. Black, red, and gold were the colors of the revolutionists.

Schurz was at the beginning of his university training in the year 1848. It was a year of tremendous import. In France King Louis Philippe had been driven out and the republic established. The day seemed to be dawning for the establishment of "German Unity," or, in other words, a "constitutional form of government on a broad democratic basis."

The Revolution soon took actual form. In Cologne the people met in the public squares to formulate their demands. All through South Germany the revolutionary spirit flamed forth. And in Austria a similar revolution demanded liberty and citizens' rights.

Meanwhile, great activity in the university town of Bonn burst forth, and Professor Kinkel, representing the citizens, declared that the liberties and rights of the German people must be granted by the princes or taken by force by the people. In Berlin, the King wavered under the flood of petitions which poured in on him, and actual fighting between the citizens and the troops, in March, 1849, resulted in the temporary acquiescence of the King in the popular demand. But the victory of the people was not followed up and proved to be short-lived.

Soon, throughout Germany, the realization began to spread that the revolution of March, which had seemed so glorious, would amount to little unless action was promptly taken. Soon also it became apparent that the King would give nothing but promises, and that the people would be no better off than before. Accordingly, in Frankfurt, Eisenach, Bonn, Dresden, and other cities, the revolutionists planned to cast off the yoke of the King, and many bloody fights took place between the people and the monarch's Prussian bayonets.

In all this Schurz and his friend Kinkel played an active part. But the power was on the side of the King, and one by one the small bands of revolutionists were defeated by the trained Prussian troops. Schurz had fought with credit in several engagements, and finally, with many other revolutionists, had taken refuge in the fortress of Rastatt, which for three weeks held out against the Prussian army that besieged it. Finally the fortress was compelled to surrender, and at great peril, Schurz and two companions escaped through a sewer and, crossing the Rhine by night, sought refuge on French soil.

The Revolution had ended in disaster and Schurz was an exile from his native land, to which he dared not return. He had fought for the cause of freedom;

he had lost all. But his life was saved. Kinkel and others of the revolutionists, less fortunate than Schurz, were condemned to life-imprisonment.

But although Schurz was free, the knowledge that Kinkel was imprisoned inspired in him the resolve to aid his friend in escaping. It was dangerous work, for it was necessary for Schurz to return in disguise to Germany, where, had he been recognized, he would immediately have suffered Kinkel's fate. But the loyalty of Schurz to his friend was rewarded by the final accomplishment of his plans; and after many exciting adventures Kinkel succeeded in his escape from prison by lowering himself at night from a window in his cell, by a rope which Schurz had smuggled in to him. And a few days later the two men succeeded in reaching the seacoast and took passage on a ship to England.

For several years Kinkel and his family lived in London, where a large number of political refugees had gathered. It was a brilliant gathering, and in these many people of varied accomplishment Carl Schurz found much to interest him. Here, too, it was that Schurz found, in the daughter of another German exile, the young woman, Margaretha Meyer, who a few months later became his wife.

The year 1852 was covered by a gloomy cloud. Throughout all Europe the Liberal movement seemed suppressed. In France, Louis Napoleon had made himself Emperor and was recognized by England; the French Republic was gone. In Italy, Mazzini had fought in vain for a united country under a free government. Kossuth had fought for the national independence of Hungary, but had gone into exile, a defeated man. In Germany, revolutionists had met a similar fate. To Carl Schurz there seemed but one direction in which he might turn. Far beyond the Atlantic the United States of America offered a republican government where the people ruled themselves by popular laws, free to live their lives and express their thoughts, free from the yokes of kings and princes. In August, 1852, Schurz and his young wife sailed for New York.

The first task which Schurz set for himself on his arrival was to learn in the shortest possible time to speak, read, and write the English language. Chiefly by reading the newspapers this task was soon accomplished, and in a very few years there were not many Americans who could claim a more exact and fluent command of their own language than he.

Schurz had come to the United States a poor man and an exile, but he was fortunate in possessing a number of friends who lived in the larger Eastern cities, and through them he obtained many valuable introductions and rapidly widened his acquaintanceship, particularly in political and literary circles.

Since the founding of the Republic slavery had existed in the United States. Particularly in the Southern states thousands of negro slaves furnished practically the only labor on the vast plantations and in the homes of the owners. Against the slowly widening influence of slavery a small band of anti-slavery men were opposing by every means at their command the growth of this condition so utterly opposed to the laws of freedom and civilization. "I saw the decisive contest rapidly approaching," wrote Schurz, "and I felt an irresistible impulse to prepare myself for usefulness, however modest, in the impending crisis: and to that end I pursued with increased assiduity my studies of the political history and the social workings of the Republic, and of the theory and practical workings of its institutions."

Schurz had German friends and relatives living in Illinois, Wisconsin, and Missouri. It seemed to him that, by visiting them, he would be enabled to see more of the country and study at first-hand the actual "real America," which he must thoroughly understand if he was to take a helpful part in the impending struggle.

During the year 1854, Schurz visited all of the large cities of the Middle West, and particularly the states of Wisconsin and Missouri, which were largely settled by Germans. The West attracted him, and after carefully considering many places, he determined to settle in the pleasant little village of Watertown, Wisconsin.

In the years of his residence in Watertown, Schurz took up the law as his profession, and at the same time began actively to participate in local politics. The large German population in the Western states was a voting power that was of great importance, and Schurz's high standing and reputation made it only natural that he should soon be chosen as their spokesman and leader.

These were stirring days. The great question of slavery was uppermost. With the entrance of new territory into the Union, the question flamed forth with greater violence: would the new states be free states or slave states? Would the slave-holders or the anti-slavery men rule the land? Would slavery or freedom dominate?

Schurz flung himself into politics and the anti-slavery party of the North. With clear vision he realized that slavery must be destroyed, but that the United States must be preserved; a separation of the slave states from the Union could not be tolerated; all must be united in freedom.

Rapidly the reputation of Carl Schurz as a political speaker spread beyond Wisconsin. He was called to address meetings in neighboring states, and finally he was summoned even to Boston, to address a great meeting in the historic Faneuil Hall. In Illinois he met Abraham Lincoln, soon to hold the office of President of the United States; everywhere he encountered the leaders in the great Republic, men of every party and every type of character; the men who were guiding the steps of the nation.

Throughout the campaign for the election of Abraham Lincoln to the presidency, Carl Schurz gave his entire energy as a speaker and organizer, and as a result soon became recognized as a person of influence in the victorious party. During these months the friendship of Schurz and Lincoln was strengthened, and other ties with other men were made, which were to have a strong influence, not only on Schurz's own life, but on the history of his adopted country.

On April 12, 1861, the storm which had so long been

brewing between the Northern and Southern states broke with the capture of Fort Sumter, in Charleston Harbor, by the Confederate forces. For some time the government of the so-called Confederate States had attempted to open negotiations with the Federal authorities for a peaceful separation. But the North had stood firm in the position that at all costs the Union must be preserved. With the fall of Sumter came the opening of the Civil War, which for four long years plunged the land in blood.

Three days later President Lincoln issued a proclamation calling for 75,000 volunteers; and on June 10 the Northern troops were repulsed at Big Bethel, and July 21, were routed at Bull Run. The long war had begun. During these first months of the war Schurz threw himself into the work of organizing in New York a regiment of German cavalry; but his services were considered of even greater value in another kind of activity, and a few weeks later he was on his way to Madrid, as United States Minister to Spain.

There is probably no other country in the world where such a rapid and spectacular progress would be possible. Ten years before, Carl Schurz was an exile from his native land, a poor newcomer to a strange country. Now, after this brief period, he was to return to Europe, the powerful representative of a great republic.

Early in 1862 Schurz returned to the United States. During the months which he had spent in Spain he had rendered valuable service in keeping the Spanish government informed of the exact condition of affairs in the United States, and impressing upon the Spanish authorities the desirability of maintaining friendly relations with the North, and an interest in the cause of freedom.

But Schurz was restless in a position of security, no matter how great its importance, while others were risking their lives for their country's cause. "I became convinced," he said, "that, in such times, the true place for a young and able-bodied man was in the field, and not in an easy-chair." Schurz laid his case before Mr. Lincoln, and the President agreed to accept his resignation and gave him a commission in the army.

At the outbreak of the war the Regular Army was very small, its officers few. Of these officers many had gone over to the army of the Confederate States. There was great need of officers for the vast volunteer armies which were being formed, and it became necessary to select men from civil life, on account of their general intelligence, and give them appointments as officers. Few of these had any military experience or particular knowledge of military science. Because of these conditions, and also because of his brief military experience in the revolutionary army of 1849, Schurz was appointed a brigadier-general for immediate service.

His experience during the Civil War included many of the famous campaigns and battles, and in all of them he played an active and important part. During the year 1862, Fort Henry and Fort Donelson were captured by the Union forces, and on March 9,

the Monitor, designed by John Ericsson, defeated the
Confederate ironclad Merrimac. Early in April General Grant won the victory of Shiloh, and on the 24th
of the same month Admiral David G. Farragut ran
the forts below New Orleans with his ships, and captured the city. In the East during this same period,
the Confederate army, under General Robert E. Lee,
pressed forward toward the city of Washington, but
was finally thrown back across the Potomac River
after the battle of Antietam.

In the following year, 1863, the Confederate army
under General Lee again marched North, but was defeated, July 1–3, at the great battle of Gettysburg.
In this battle Schurz took part, and from the crest of
Cemetery Hill watched the Confederate infantry of
General Pickett make their brave charge against the
Union forces. Fifteen thousand strong, in a long close
line, with bayonets gleaming in the sunshine and flags
waving in the breeze, the gray-clad soldiers of the
Confederacy appeared from the dark shadows of the
woods and came steadily across a mile of open fields.
Under a tremendous fire from the Union artillery the
gray line slowly melted as it advanced, leaving the
soft green of the meadow flecked with gray-clad
bodies of dead and wounded. Closing the gaps, they
came steadily on, now lost behind a low rise of ground,
now again in view, their flags still flying above them.
Then, within rifle-range, a cloud of smoke lifted like
fog from the Union guns, and as it floated off on the
light wind, the Union soldiers saw the remnant of
Pickett's brave band slowly retreating from the field.

Although more than a year of war was to follow, the strength of the Southern offensive was shattered.

On July 4, Vicksburg surrendered to Grant, and in November came the victories of Lookout Mountain and Missionary Ridge. In the following year were other victories in the battles of the Wilderness and Spottsylvania. Another drive of the Confederates against Washington was attempted by General Early, but he was defeated by General Sheridan in three battles and was forced to withdraw. Then came the capture of Atlanta and General Sherman's famous march through Georgia to the sea. On the water were achieved the victory of the Kearsarge over the Confederate steamer Alabama, and Admiral Farragut's successful passage of the forts at Mobile Bay. In April of the year 1865 came the complete surrender of the armies of the Confederacy. The Union was preserved; slavery was destroyed.

With the ending of the war, Schurz began again to take an active part in the political life of the nation, and for a time devoted himself to a study of the perplexing difficulties which surrounded the reconstruction of the South, impoverished by years of war and economically ruined by the emancipation of the slaves.

In the autumn of 1867 he again visited Germany. The high position which he now held in the great Republic assured him of a welcome, but the attentions which were heaped upon him were a particular tribute to the man who had once fled by night. Bismarck, "The Minister" of Germany, honored him by inviting him to long conferences, in which he eagerly questioned Schurz concerning the great war in which he had taken part, and asked many questions about the political and social conditions of the Republic of which Schurz had become a citizen.

On his return to the United States, Schurz was elected to the United States Senate, representing the great state of Missouri, where he had now taken up his residence. "I remember vividly the feelings which almost oppressed me when I first sat down in my chair in the Senate Chamber. Now I had actually reached a most exalted public position, to which my boldest dreams of ambition had hardly dared to aspire. I was still a young man, just forty. Little more than sixteen years had elapsed since I had landed on these shores a homeless waif, saved from the wreck of a revolutionary movement in Europe. Then I was enfolded in the generous hospitality of the American people, opening to me, as freely as to its own children, the great opportunities of the new world. And here I was now, a member of the highest law-making body of the greatest of republics."

But a still greater honor was to come. With the election of President Hayes in 1877, Schurz became the Secretary of the Interior of the United States. In this high position his ability found ample room for exercise, and the reforms which he in large measure effected, both in the civil-service system of appointment — by which men were placed in government positions as a result of examination on their merits, as opposed to their appointment regardless of merit but as a political reward — and in the Bureau of Indian Affairs, were of unusual value to the nation.

On leaving the Department of the Interior at the close of President Hayes's administration, Schurz was confronted by an almost embarrassing number of positions for his future occupation. For a time he occupied an editorial position on the New York *Evening Post;* but he still continued to take an active and important part in the politics of the day. For some years after his retirement from the *Post* he devoted himself to literature, and produced, among other books, a life of Henry Clay which won high commendation.

After a brief business episode, he again returned to the field of journalism, and for six years contributed weekly the leading editorial to *Harper's Weekly.* Once again he visited Europe; but old age was growing heavy on his shoulders, and on his return to the United States he retired each year a little more from the active fields of politics and journalism which had so long held him, and to which he had so gladly contributed.

On May 14, 1906, surrounded by his children, the end came. "Es ist so einfach zu sterben" (it is so simple to die), was his farewell to those about him. As he lived, so did he die, simply and unafraid.

V

THEODORE THOMAS

Born in Essen, Germany, 1835
Died in Chicago, 1905

CIVILIZATION is a condition of organization; in a nation it is a name for progress and enlightenment. Literature, art, music, and science are measures of civilization; so also are agricultural, industrial, and social progress. All men contributing to the advancement of civilization are benefactors of mankind. The inventor, the artist, the physician, the scientist, the manufacturer, the writer, the explorer, and the musician, all contribute to human happiness and advancement.

No man who lives for himself alone can add to the progress of the world. Only they who unselfishly have lived for others deserve the gratitude of their fellow men. And it is encouraging that, in almost every case, those men who have accomplished most have sooner or later received their high rewards.

Probably no nation in all the world has given so much in so short a time to civilization as the United States. The reason is not far to seek, for in no other country have such opportunities to accomplish their fine desires ever been offered to men of ambition and ability; never has there been so fair a field in which each man might rise as high as his own strength would carry him.

Since the world began, music has been a part of the very life of every nation. As labor in the shop and field and mine have produced the material things so necessary for the health and comfort of the body, so, for the development of the mind and for the happiness of all people, have painters, sculptors, and musicians contributed their fairest conceptions, that life might be more beautiful and the world a better place to live in for all mankind.

In the older European countries music has been handed down for centuries from father to son. In conditions where music has so completely become a part of life, great musicians from time to time have lived and left their lasting contributions. In the older civilizations there was a fertile field long cultivated for the ever-increasing growth of music.

In the United States, however, another condition existed. Here was a new civilization, transplanted by early settlers from beyond the sea. Here there was no existing civilization developed through centuries. It was a land to which had come men and women from every nation in the world, seeking freedom from the rule of kings and a place where they might live in peace and equality, regardless of their birth. Each brought with him the civilization of his native land. But much was lost in the migration; there was no place, at first, for many elements of European civilization in the busy life of the new world.

For half a century, from the glorious day when the United States cast off the yoke of a European monarchy and became a republic, there was small time in

the lives of Americans for music, art, and all the other
finer elements of civilization. It was necessary that
men should explore and open up the vast rich country
in which they lived. They must build cities and plant
fields with grain; they must dig deep mines and find
coal and metals, and they must cut timber from the
forests for the needs of the nation. Also, they found
it necessary to develop the government of their new
nation, and form from the wilderness, where once only
the Indians dwelt, new states to increase the union of
the great Republic.

But through all these years of labor there remained
in the minds of men an appreciation of those other
more beautiful factors of civilization; memories of an
inheritance that were like dreams from which these
pioneers waited to be awakened by someone who, at
the right time, would come to them and, understand-
ingly, would point out the way. The love of music
was in their hearts.

Meanwhile, in the town of Essen, in Germany, by
the North Sea, was born, on the eleventh of October,
1835, a boy, Theodore Thomas, who in a few short
years was destined to bring to the great United States
that appreciation of music of which it was now so
thoroughly unconscious.

The boy's father was the Stadtpfeifer, or town musician, of Essen. It was a position of honor, for the
Stadtpfeifer played on all important occasions, and
many great musicians have held this title.

From infancy the boy showed an aptitude for music. At the age of five he played the violin in public,

and he spent as much of his play-time as he could with his father's orchestra, playing his violin and reading all the new music he could find.

When he was ten years old, the family emigrated to America. It was the land of promise, and a bigger and brighter future seemed to await them in the vast free United States than in the sleepy German village where for generations their ancestors had been born and lived and died.

This was before the days of fast steamships; then the passage of the Atlantic was made in sailing vessels, and often the voyage lasted as many weeks as now it is measured by days. The Thomas family found passage on an American vessel; and it was six long weeks after their departure that they landed, on a hot July morning in the year 1845, in the city of New York.

There was little or no real music in the United States. A few people played the piano or cornet, there were a number of brass bands, and some of the theatres boasted of a few musicians, but orchestras and good music were unknown.

The Thomas family was a large one, and the father worked far into the night, playing in theatre orchestras, to provide for his wife and children. It was only natural that young Theodore, with his musical talent, should be called upon to help; and so almost from the beginning the boy labored with the father, playing his violin in various theatres, at a dancing-school, and wherever he could earn an honest dollar.

Three years later the father enlisted in a navy band,

and the boy followed him, playing second horn to the father's first. But a year later, both father and son left the navy; and as the former was now able alone to provide for the family, young Theodore found himself free to carry out his own plans and lay the foundations for his future.

With a little box of clothing, his violin, and a bundle of posters announcing a concert by "Master T-T," Theodore set out alone to try his fortune with the world. For a year he wandered through the Southern states, giving his concerts in hotel dining-rooms, in schoolhouses, or wherever he considered it possible to gather an audience. As the people arrived, Theodore would stand at the door and take in the money; then, when he thought that all who were coming were present, he would hurry to the front of the hall and begin the concert.

A year later he was back again in New York, poor in pocket but rich in experience of the world. "I was then fifteen years old," he later wrote, "and somehow had recognized the necessity of studying if I expected to accomplish anything in this world. But what? I did not know, of course, that a general education was needed, or even what it meant. My first idea was to become a virtuoso, so I began to practise and play in concerts."

Shortly after his return to New York, the fifteen-year-old boy was engaged as the leading violinist in the orchestra of a German theatre. But this experience gave him more than an actual living; for here he became acquainted with the plays of the great Ger-

man poets and masters of literature, and he also widened his musical horizon far beyond the rather limited
boundaries which had up to that time confined it.

During the next two or three years his musical education prospered. Great singers and musicians began
occasionally to visit America: Jenny Lind, Sontag,
Mario, Grisi, Bosio, and Alboni. Thomas played
everywhere in concerts and operas, and this gave him
constant opportunity to hear these artists under the
best of conditions. "The pure and musical quality of
their art," he has said, "was of great value in forming
the taste of an impressionable boy at the outset of his
career." The influence of this experience did much to
prepare him for his own triumphs in coming years.

There were at that time no real orchestras in America. An orchestra meant to Thomas a selected organization of skilled musicians "sufficiently subsidized to
enable it to hold the rehearsals necessary for artistic
performances, its object and aim to be to attain the
highest artistic performance of master-works." Of the
existing orchestras of the time all were of negligible
quality, and their leaders mere "time-beaters," instead of true musicians.

But at this time such a leader appeared for a short
period in the circle of Thomas's life. Karl Eckert, the
leader of the orchestra accompanying Mademoiselle
Sontag, appeared in New York, and Thomas secured
a position as one of the first violinists in the orchestra,
a position from which he was soon promoted to leader
of the second violins. Thomas gave his best effort to
his new work. It was a place of responsibility, and the

boy was young, but he saw his opportunity, grasped it, and held it.

The following year Thomas won promotion to *Konzert-meister*, or leader of the first violins; and here his extreme genius became the more apparent, for he was now the leader of men many of whom were old enough to be his father. This was the definite beginning of his career, for the experience of playing in a well-organized orchestra gave him a thorough schooling, not only in his duties as Konzert-meister but — and this was of particular value to him — in the practical business side of orchestral management.

In 1853 his education was further broadened by a year in the orchestra of Jullien, a famous European conductor. This was the first time that he had heard or played in a large and complete orchestra, and the result was that he was now ready to step out from the ranks and begin to develop his ability as an individual and a leader.

For about twelve years the New York Philharmonic Society had struggled, against popular indifference, to create a source of real music in the community. In 1854 Thomas was elected a member. He was nineteen years old. For thirty-six years he was destined to hold a more or less close association with it, first as violinist and later as its leader.

In the year 1855 William Mason, "a refined, sincere and highly educated musician," organized a quartette of string players. Thomas was invited to play first violin, although he was the youngest member of the quartette. Mason played the piano, and the other members were Carl Bergmann, J. Mosenthal, and G. Matzka. It was an association of true artists, and its influence was of great consequence to Thomas in the opportunity which it afforded for the expression of his art and in the lasting friendships which it formed.

The concerts which were given by the quartette were known as "chamber concerts," and the programmes included only the best music for the string quartette, or for a sonata or trio with piano accompaniment. Three mornings a week were given up to rehearsals, and as only six programmes were arranged for the year's repertoire, the deep interest and enthusiasm of all the members is apparent. "It was this exhaustive study of master-works, especially those of Beethoven, continued through fourteen years, which gave Thomas his mastery of the string choir of the orchestra, and his profound insight into the classical school of music."

The first experience of Theodore Thomas in conducting an opera is characteristic of the man and illustrates his fine self-confidence and his instant acceptance of opportunity. One evening he came home from his work and settled down in an easy chair for a few hours of rest and relaxation. A few blocks away, at the Academy of Music, an opera (Halévy's "Jewess") was to be sung. The house was filled and an impatient audience waited for the curtain: but the conductor was ill, and there was no one to take his place. Someone thought of Thomas, and a messenger was sent to ask him if he would conduct the opera. Thomas had never before conducted an opera; he was wholly unfamiliar with the one in question. But his answer was an immediate "I will." And he did, with complete success.

But the limitations of the opera, the Philharmonic, and the quartette could not satisfy him, and in 1862, for the first time, he announced an orchestral concert under his own direction. This was the first "Thomas concert." The orchestra consisted of about forty players. In the programme it is interesting to read the titles of two compositions which had never before been played in America. Here was the intimation of his life-policy of giving his American audience the best current music, often before it was completely recognized in the Old World.

"In 1862 I concluded to devote my energies to the cultivation of the public taste for instrumental music. Our chamber concerts had created a spasmodic interest, our programmes were reprinted as models of their kind, even in Europe, and our performances had reached a high standard. As concert violinist, I was at that time popular, and played much. But what this country needed most of all to make it musical, was a good orchestra, and plenty of concerts within the reach of the people."

After several seasons of occasional concerts, Thomas determined to organize an orchestra of his own. There was no endowment, there were no backers. All the responsibility of organization and finance fell on the shoulders of the young leader. The orchestra was called the "Theodore Thomas Orchestra," and it was truly his, in name and fact. With a firm determination to bring the highest form of music to the people and to teach them thoroughly to enjoy it, he began a regular series of evening concerts; and after a season of moderate success, he inaugurated a series of Summer-Night concerts, given in the open air in a park in the city.

The life-work of Theodore Thomas was begun; the little violin-player from an obscure foreign village was fast assuming the musical leadership of a nation — a nation to which he gave musical standards and an understanding of his art.

In the next few years a number of important events brightened the steady work which had become now necessary to his success. The leadership of the Brooklyn Philharmonic Society was awarded him, a position of high honor which enabled him to employ his own orchestra in a series of twenty additional concerts. His marriage to Miss Minna L. Rhodes, an event which brought into his life much happiness and an influence which did much to hasten the development of his rare abilities, occurred during this period. Finally, in 1867, a short trip to Europe became possible; and at London, Paris, Munich, Vienna, Dresden, and Berlin he listened to the performances of the most celebrated European orchestras and gained much by comparison of them with his own. Moreover, on his return to the United States, he was enabled to give to his audiences the most modern music played as he had heard it under the leadership of the composers themselves.

The thought has often occurred, Why did not

Theodore Thomas himself become a composer? To be sure, on a few occasions compositions of his own were given to the public, but this happened only during his earlier career. The answer may be quoted in his own words: "As a young man I wished to be a composer, but circumstances forced me into the executant's career. My creative vein was worthy of development had I had the time for it, but it fell short of genius, and I believed I could do more for my art and my country by familiarizing the people with the literature already created than by adding to it myself. The exacting nature of my work in the orchestra required all my time and strength, and made another kind of serious work impossible; and as long as I could not give the time necessary to produce compositions which would be satisfactory to myself, I preferred to let it alone altogether."

The winter concerts and the Summer-Night concerts in the Central Park Garden were continued; but the revenue from the winter concerts fell short of the sum which the expenses of the organization required, and in 1868 Thomas decided to give them up and play in New York City in the summer only. During the winter months he planned to carry his orchestra about the country, and by playing in all the larger cities, not only assure himself of larger houses, but at the same time widen the scope of the musical education which he longed to afford the entire country.

Beginning in the year 1869, for twenty-two years Thomas toured the length and breadth of the land. The Southern states and New England heard his rare programmes; San Francisco and Montreal anticipated with eagerness his next arrival; and even to the new frontier lands of Texas the tireless conductor led his little company of musicians. For years identified with New York City, he now became a national figure, an individual who had given himself to and was claimed by the entire country.

Among the first cities to give him recognition were Boston and Cincinnati. In the former city a musical critic wrote: "The visit of this famous orchestra has given our music-lovers a new and quick sensation. Boston has not heard such performances before. We thank Mr. Thomas for setting palpably before us a higher ideal of orchestral execution." In Cincinnati music had long been an important part of the life of the city. "We have not seen at any time audiences so wrought upon as those that attended the concerts of Theodore Thomas"; and "the finest orchestral music that has ever been given in this city," wrote the newspapers. It was the same everywhere: wherever the orchestra played, praise unstinted was accorded.

During this period of his life Thomas devoted a considerable part of his energies to the conducting of "festivals" in the large cities of the country. These festivals were elaborately planned musical programmes, in which the orchestra and often several hundred voices took part. The festivals were in some cities annual affairs, in which the local singing societies coöperated. The festivals held in New York, Cincinnati, and Chicago were particularly popular, and their success and popularity may be truly said to have been almost entirely due to the untiring work of their great conductor.

But success and recognition in the lives of great men rarely come without compensating failures and disappointments; and in the life of Theodore Thomas were many days when failure seemed to be his chief reward. The great Chicago fire in 1871, which destroyed almost the entire city, caused him a financial loss that he was hardly able to bear. Then, in 1876, came the Philadelphia Centennial Exposition, commemorating the hundredth anniversary of the founding of the United States. A great musical programme was planned and Thomas was honored with its entire direction. But the crowds visiting the exposition did not appreciate the concerts, and to the deep disappointment of Thomas and the committee behind the plan, they were so poorly attended that it was soon necessary to abandon them. This was a hard blow to Thomas. He had lost much money on account of the Chicago disaster, and now this new calamity increased the losses which he could ill afford. Financial ruin faced him. His large and valuable musical library, his only asset, was seized by the sheriff to pay the debts of the orchestra. The library consisted of musical scores, collected throughout a lifetime, without which he could not conduct his orchestra. Only the kindness of a loyal friend, who bought up the library and gave it back to Thomas several years later, saved him from complete disaster. As it was, he might well have gone into bankruptcy and settled his debts; but his fine sense of honor prevailed, and he preferred to assume his responsibilities in full and meet them in their entirety in later years.

In 1878 he received an offer to establish and direct a college of music which a number of influential and wealthy men proposed to found in the city of Cincinnati. Thomas gladly undertook the directorship, and a splendid institution developed under his wise guidance; but the scheme which he planned was greater than the board of directors desired; and, seeing that it would be impossible for him to carry out his complete plans, he resigned from his office in 1880 and returned to his former work as an orchestra leader.

Another trip to Europe brightened the gloom which had surrounded the recent years of disappointment, and the recognition which now began to be accorded him helped to bring back his spirit of optimism for the future. The conductorship of the London Philharmonic Society was offered to him; a high honor which only his love for his adopted country forced him to refuse. In the same year the honorary degree of Doctor of Music, "by way of recognition of the substantial service which he has rendered to musical culture in the United States," was conferred upon him by Yale University. Other universities later conferred similar degrees, and of the many honors which came to him there were none which he more highly prized.

The next few years were years of triumph, for during this period Thomas devoted himself to the management of great musical festivals in New York, Cincinnati, and Chicago, and finally, in 1885, conducted a festival tour from New York to San Francisco.

Another financial setback came now, hard on the heels of this period of success, for he was induced to accept the musical leadership of an American opera company, an enterprise which seemed to contain every necessary element for success. But after a short life the entire project proved itself a failure, and once again Thomas returned to the orchestra, which for the rest of his life he was destined never again to leave. In 1889 the death of his wife came as another blow which seemed impossible, for the time, to bear. But a new and final period in his life was already dawning, a period of recognition and accomplishment.

Theodore Thomas had once said: " Chicago is the only city on the continent, except New York, where there is sufficient musical culture to enable me to give a series of fifty successive concerts." In 1881 a permanent orchestra was established in Boston, and Chicago became ambitious to follow the example. The leadership of the new Chicago orchestra was offered to Thomas. New York had in a large measure failed to fulfill his expectations. But what New York would not provide, Chicago offered. The opportunity could not be refused, and Thomas accepted.

Conditions for the founding of a permanent Chicago orchestra were far from favorable. There was no building suitable for orchestral purposes; the cultivated class of the population was small, and, moreover, the city did not afford musicians of a quality suited for the formation of the orchestra. But Thomas throve on adversity. From New York he imported sixty musicians, of whom half a dozen had been members of the old New York Thomas Orchestra, and with thirty selected Chicago players he completed the necessary quota of ninety men. Concerts were given in buildings unsuited for this kind of entertainment, under the most trying conditions, but the public was taught to undertsand the worth of the great undertaking by the most carefully arranged programmes.

Success came at last. For a period the expenses of the orchestra were carried by a number of liberal and far-sighted citizens; but finally it was decided to find out how sincerely such music was actually desired by the people. A general appeal for an endowment fund was made, the fund to be invested in a suitable home for the orchestra.

The result was far beyond the wildest hopes of the projectors of the plan. In less than a year almost $700,000 was subscribed by over eight thousand subscribers, from every corner of the vast city, from every class of society, from rich and from poor.

It was the realization of the dream of Thomas's youth. The home of the Thomas Orchestra was dedicated in 1904. This building, contributed by the people that the music which he had brought into their lives might become a part of their existence, is his monument, which will long endure. But more lasting than those walls of stone is the recognition which history will accord to him who in his way made the world a better living-place for his countrymen.

Theodore Thomas died in the year that followed the dedication of the home of his orchestra. The fourteen final years of his life had found in Chicago the material

appreciation which he deserved. A second marriage —
this time to Miss Rose Fay — brought him its happiness. With no precedents, no traditions, and no experience of others to guide him, he had done the kind
of work for music in the United States that the first
settlers had done when they ploughed their first furrows in the wilderness. He had blazed the trail; he
had opened the way that others might follow on.

"German-born, associated with German musicians
all through his life, meeting them daily, and living as
it were in a German atmosphere, yet he was the
strongest of Americans in sentiment, disposition, feeling and patriotism. Many a time have I heard him
resent foreign slurs upon American institutions, and
defend the national government's policy against its
critics. His love for the United States, where he had
lived from boyhood, and his respect and admiration
for the broad-minded views of its people as well as
their public spirit, was deep, hearty, and sincere."
Such was Theodore Thomas in the estimation of one
who knew him well.

His creed was simple, but it was a creed from which
he never deviated. "Throughout my life my aim has
been to make good music popular, and now it appears
that I have only done the public justice in believing,
and acting constantly on the belief, that the people
would enjoy and support the best in art when continually set before them in a clear and intelligent
manner."

VI

ANDREW CARNEGIE

Born in Dunfermline, Scotland, 1835
Died in Lenox, Massachusetts, 1919

THE little town of Dunfermline in Scotland has for centuries been famous for its weaving. For generations have the sturdy inhabitants devoted their lives to the looms. And here, in this quiet and humble corner of the busy world, was born, on the twenty-fifth of November, 1835, a small baby whom his parents named Andrew, who was destined to become one of the richest men that the world has seen, a citizen of the United States, a world philanthropist, and a true captain of industry. So simply was Andrew Carnegie born into the tremendous nineteenth century.

Andrew's father was a weaver of damasks, as had been his father and grandfathers for generations back in the Carnegie history; and the boy was doubtless expected by his parents to carry on the established vocation of the family. But, as so often happens, circumstances unforeseen and impossible to anticipate abruptly changed the whole life-work of a community, and in the change the small boy's life was directed into a new channel which was destined to bring him the greatest material rewards. The Carnegies wove with hand-looms. Suddenly, invention gave the power-loom to the world. Gone immediately was the demand for the now more costly product of skilled and patient fingers. The swift machines destroyed a trade to build an industry, and in the destruction the Carnegie family was swept into new work and a new environment.

With his only means of earning a living destroyed, necessity compelled the elder Carnegie to seek occupation somewhere beyond the limits of the quiet Scotch town. Across the Atlantic a great new republic was just reaching its young manhood. Its fast-sailing clippers had made the Stars and Stripes of its flag known on every sea, and tales of the daring Yankee skippers had brought to complacent England a rude awakening from her peaceful sense of maritime supremacy. Within its boundaries even greater developments were taking form under the firm hands of the Americans. A rich inland empire was disclosing wealth beyond dreams of men: mines of iron and coal and various metals, forests unexplored and seemingly limitless, millions of rich acres unturned by the ploughshare and destined in time to come to feed the world. Already minds of vision were organizing railroads to bring together these riches and to make them accessible to the nation as a whole. All over the world people were turning from war-scarred and time-worn nations oppressed by the rule of kings to this free land of promise. Men and women and little children crossed the broad Atlantic to live happily in a country where men ruled themselves by self-imposed laws, and where education gave to all an equal opportunity. And with these went also the

Andrew Carnegie

Carnegie family, to add their sturdy strength to the great Republic.

There were four in the little family — the father, mother, and two boys, Andrew and Thomas. Andrew was thirteen years old and his brother four when this great life-changing event occurred — too young to realize its significance or to find in it much else but the romance and adventure of a sea-voyage and the excitement of seeing new places and strange faces. There was a considerable cotton manufacture in Allegheny City, Pennsylvania, and there the Carnegie family settled, in a neighborhood known as Barefoot Square in a part of the city called Slabtown. Andrew was old enough to work, and money was needed to meet the higher costs of living in this new land; so both father and son found work in the same cotton mill, Andrew as a bobbin-boy at a wage of $1.20 a week.

This was the first step in Andrew's career, and other steps came with what seemed a marked rapidity. But it was not that unusual opportunities confronted the lad; on the contrary, nothing could have seemed to offer a more slender promise than the arduous and elementary work which he gladly accepted. The promise lay rather in the boy; and, as is ever the case, Andrew was in those early years proving the old truism that the right kind of a boy rises above adversity and grows strong by battling with discouragement.

Andrew was soon promoted, at a slight increase in pay, to be engineer's assistant in the factory. For twelve long hours each day he shoveled coal under the boilers and ran the engine. His pay was now $1.80 a week, and all of it went into the family purse; for not only was all the money earned by father and son required for the household expenses, but Mrs. Carnegie added her mite by taking in washing from the neighbors. And it is interesting to recollect that of these neighbors one named Phipps, a shoemaker, had a son Harry, a chum of Andrew's, who also, in later years, became a man of wealth and importance in the nation's business affairs.

A year later Andrew again made an advance; for, leaving his work in the cellar of the factory, he took a job as district messenger boy for the telegraph company, at $3.00 a week. Now came an opportunity which his conscientious study enabled him to grasp. Ever since he had obtained his job with the telegraph company he had studied telegraphy and spent all his spare time in practice. "My entrance into the telegraph office," he once said, "was a transition from darkness to light — from firing a small engine in a dirty cellar into a clean office with bright windows and a literary atmosphere; with books, newspapers, pens, and pencils all around me, I was the happiest boy alive." One morning, before the telegraph operator reached the office, a message was signaled from Philadelphia. Andrew was always early at work, and although the boys were not supposed to know anything about the instruments or allowed to touch them, he jumped to the receiver and took down the message with accuracy. His resourcefulness and willingness to assume responsibility were immediately recognized, and he was promoted to operator, at a salary of $300 a year.

In addition to his study of telegraphy Andrew, during this period, became a constant reader of good books. A gentleman living in the neighborhood had opened his private library to Andrew and a few other boys every week-end, and gave them permission to take certain books home with them. Andrew made full use of the opportunity. "Only he who has longed as I did for Saturdays to come," he said in after years, "can understand what Colonel Anderson did for me and the boys of Allegheny. Is it any wonder that I resolved, if ever surplus wealth came to me, I would use it imitating my benefactor?"

The boy's earnest attention to his work was not long unnoticed, and the divisional superintendent of the Pennsylvania Railroad, hearing of his quickness and enthusiasm, appointed him railway operator in his own office, increasing his salary to $35 a month. A second opportunity to assume responsibility occurred. During the superintendent's absence from the office early one morning, an accident was reported on one of the lines, which tied up the road and threatened a costly blockade. Andrew at once took charge of the situation, and knowing exactly what the superintendent would do in such a situation, wrote out the necessary orders, to which he signed the superintendent's name, to set the trains again in motion, and straightened out the whole difficulty. When his chief arrived, Andrew reported what he had done. The superintendent said nothing to him, but to the president

of the railroad he wrote that he "had a little Scotch-
man in his office who would run the whole road if they
would only give him a chance."

When Andrew was sixteen his father died, and the
boy became the head of the family; and it was at this
time that he made his first investment, although it
was necessary, with his mother's help, to borrow the
required money.

"One day Mr. Scott [the superintendent of his divi-
sion], who was the kindest of men and had taken a
great fancy to me, asked if I had or could find five
hundred dollars to invest. . . . I answered promptly:

"'Yes, sir, I think I can.'

"'Very well,' he said, 'get it. A man has just died
who owns ten shares in the Adams Express Company,
that I want you to buy. It will cost you sixty dollars a
share. I will advance the remaining hundred dollars.'

"The matter was laid before the council of three
that night and the oracle spoke. 'Must be done.
Mortgage our house. I will take the steamer in the
morning for Ohio and see uncle and ask him to ar-
range it. I am sure he can.' Of course her visit was
successful — where did she ever fail?

"The money was procured; paid over; ten shares of
Adams Express Company stock was mine, but no one
knew our little home had been mortgaged 'to give our
boy a start.'

"Adams Express then paid monthly dividends of
one per cent, and the first check arrived. . . .

"The next day being Sunday, we boys — myself
and my ever-constant companions — took our usual

Sunday afternoon stroll in the country, and sitting down in the woods I showed them this check, saying, 'Eureka! I have found it.'

"Here was something new to all of us, for none of us had ever received anything but from toil. A return from capital was something strange and new."

Concentrating his entire efforts on his work, Andrew learned all that there was to know about train-dispatching and began to improve on the existing methods. Time passed, and Colonel Scott becoming vice-president of the railroad, Andrew promptly stepped into the position of division superintendent which Colonel Scott vacated. Carnegie was now twenty-eight years old and by careful saving and investment he had acquired a tidy capital. A chance to invest in one of the first sleeping-car companies had been accepted by him, and a large profit was ultimately made out of the investment, although at the time Carnegie had to borrow the money for the stock of a banker in Altoona and repay the loan at the rate of $15 a month. A fortunate speculation in oil, which his savings permitted him to make, gave him his first real profit, and put him immediately in a position to play with larger affairs in a larger way.

In the year 1865 Carnegie was thirty years old. As division superintendent of the Pennsylvania he had won for himself a place from which he could view a wider horizon; a large field of opportunities was visible. Also, he had saved his money; he was in a position to seize an opportunity when it appeared.

During the great Civil War Carnegie had been put

8

in charge of the government telegraph and had done well the important work which fell to him. But with the close of the war and the beginning of the period of reconstruction, he saw a greater field for the exercise of his business abilities. Iron was in great demand. Carnegie had already been active in the foundation of a mill for the production of structural iron; for three years the company had stood on the brink of failure; but Carnegie was not a "quitter," and he hung on to his faith. Now, with his brother and several other partners, he formed the Union Iron Mills. The profits were enormous. Vast railroad development throughout the country required rails and structural iron. Steel rails were worth from $90 to $100 a ton. The manufacture of steel seemed to offer even greater prospects than iron.

In 1868 Carnegie visited England. In the early days of the nineteenth century England controlled the iron business of the world; and when Carnegie made his first trip abroad, there were fifty-nine Bessemer Steel plants in Europe and only three in the United States. To-day, the United States produces over two fifths of all the steel and iron in the world, and the beginning of this great American industry can be found in the enterprise of the son of the poor Scotch weaver.

Carnegie had faith in steel. By the Bessemer process steel of high quality was economically produced by decarbonizing cast iron by forcing a blast of air through the mass of metal when it is in a molten condition. Carnegie saw the merits of this process, brought the idea home with him, and adopted it in his mills. The vindication of his faith was immediate. In an incredibly short time he had obtained control of seven great plants in the vicinity of Pittsburgh: the Homestead, the Edgar Thomson, the Duquesne Steel Works and Furnaces, the Lucy Furnaces, the Keystone Bridge Works, the Upper and Lower Union Rolling Mills. In the town to which he had come a poor lad from a foreign land, Carnegie was now assuming the proportions of a giant of industry.

Nothing was too good or too costly for the perfecting of the industry. "Carnegie was the first steelmaker in any country who flung good machinery on the scrap heap because something better had been invented. He was the first to employ a salaried chemist, and to appreciate science in its relation to manufacturing. In his early days he was the biggest borrower in Pennsylvania; and when the profits grew large they were poured back, to fertilize the soil from whence they grew. . . . So it is clear that, primarily, the aim of Andrew Carnegie was not to make large dividends or to sell stock, but to establish a solid and enduring industrial structure. First of all, he was a business builder; and the present unequaled prosperity in our iron and steel trade is largely due to the fact that American steel-makers have adopted the Carnegie policy of ranking improvements above dividends."

To protect the supply of coal which his vast steel manufacture now required, in 1889 Carnegie joined forces with Henry C. Frick, who dominated the coke-making industry. As a result, his companies soon "owned and controlled mines producing 6,000,000

tons of ore annually; 40,000 acres of coal land, and
12,000 coke ovens; steamship lines for transporting
ore to Lake Erie ports; docks for handling ore and
coal, and a railroad from Lake Erie to Pittsburgh;
70,000 acres of natural-gas territory, with 200 miles of
pipe-line; nineteen blast furnaces and five steel mills,
producing and finishing 3,250,000 tons of steel annually. The pay-roll of the year exceeded $18,000,000."

Gradually consolidating his interests, Carnegie
formed in 1890, the Carnegie Company, with a paid up
capital of $160,000,000, and in 1899 his interests were
merged into the Carnegie Steel Company. Although
still as active in affairs as ever, Carnegie now determined to retire from active business. In an address
delivered at Pittsburgh he gave his reasons. "An
opportunity to retire from business came to me un-
sought, which I considered it my duty to accept. My
resolve was made in youth to retire before old age.
From what I have seen around me, I cannot doubt the
wisdom of this course, although the change is great,
even serious, and seldom brings happiness. But this is
because so many, having abundance to retire upon,
have so little to retire to. I have always felt that old
age should be spent, not as the Scotch say, in 'making
mickle mair,' but in making good use of what has been
acquired; and I hope my friends will approve of my
action in retiring while still in full health and vigor,
and I can reasonably expect many years of usefulness
in fields which have other than personal aims."

The "opportunity" to which Carnegie referred was
the merging, in 1901, of the Carnegie Steel Company

into the United States Steel Corporation. For his personal interest Carnegie received $420,000,000.

Freed from business, the iron-master turned to follow the paths to which his idealism had constantly called him. Always a reader and a student of books, he now found himself able to make, through public libraries, books everywhere available, and in various cities and towns he contributed for library buildings more than $60,000,000. Still further to advance education and bring its advantages to all who sought it, he made other gifts, consisting of $24,000,000 to the Institute at Pittsburgh, $22,000,000 to the Carnegie Institute in Washington, and $10,000,000 to the Universities of Scotland. At the time of his death in 1919, it was estimated that he had given away to education and other worthy causes over $350,000,000.

Behind this generous distribution of his great wealth was a desire to distribute his fortune before his death. "The day is not far distant," he once said, "when the man who dies leaving behind him available wealth which was free to him to administer during life, will pass away 'unwept, unhonored and unsung,' no matter to what use he leaves the dross that he cannot take away with him. Of such the public verdict will be: 'The man who dies thus rich, dies disgraced.'"

Many other worthy causes held Carnegie's interest from his retirement from business to his death. Of all his public activities, he took perhaps greatest interest in the cause of world peace. He believed in arbitration instead of war, and aided in the organization of various leagues and commissions to that end.

But although Carnegie was one of the world's most generous givers he had no desire to abolish poverty. "We should," he said, "be quite willing to abolish luxury, but to abolish honest, industrious, self-denying poverty would be to destroy the soil upon which mankind produces the virtues which enable our race to reach a still higher civilization than it now possesses." Not to help men were his millions given, but to help men to help themselves. In his long list of philanthropies, education is the goal. "Nothing for the submerged," was his motto; but for the boy or man who honestly strove to force his way upward Carnegie would give all.

During the latter years of his life honors came to him. He was made Lord Rector of the University of St. Andrews, Edinburgh, in 1903, and received from the same university the degree of Doctor of Laws in 1905. In 1907 France made him a Commander of the Legion of Honor, and in the same year the Queen of Holland conferred on him the Order of Orange-Nassau. By his adopted country he was held in high regard, and among other honors was made an honorary alumnus of the University of Princeton.

Simple, as his parents had been before him, in spite of his vast wealth which opened the world to him, Carnegie desired that the world should know his pride in his own hard struggle and in the poverty of his birth. On the crest which he designed for himself is a weaver's shuttle, indicating his father's occupation, and there is a coronet turned upside down, surmounted by a liberty cap, and supported by American and

Scots flags. The motto is "Death to Privilege." To radical minds there is food for thought in this strange crest and its motto, for they who cry death to privilege often mean death to ambition, and without ambition the son of the weaver would never have become the world benefactor who made himself able to give wealth by the hundreds of millions for the good of humanity.

On the day following his death, in the summer of 1919, a great New York newspaper began an account of his life with these paragraphs, a final tribute to an American by adoption: —

"Andrew Carnegie, the outstanding figure of nineteenth-century industrialism, will go down through the ages as the very personification of 'Triumphant Democracy.'

"Overcoming almost insuperable obstacles by his unusual energy and sheer tenacity of purpose, Andrew Carnegie rose from a humble messenger-boy to wealth beyond the dreams of avarice. He rose from obscurity to a unique position in the world.

"Yet despite the tremendous effort put into everything he undertook, Andrew Carnegie's meteoric rise was due entirely to the opportunity offered to all in a land of freedom and of free speech. This fact he emphasized in all his writings, and in all his speeches. Moreover, it had a profound effect upon the course he adopted for the administration of his vast fortune, for the development of mankind, and the furtherance of science."

VII

JAMES J. HILL

Born near Guelph, Ontario, Canada, 1837
Died in St. Paul, Minnesota, 1916

A HUNDRED years ago Napoleon, with the sword, carved out of Europe an empire. To accomplish this, the lives of men by the thousand were sacrificed. With misery and bloodshed its boundaries were extended, and in a few years it had vanished into the history of the past. In like manner, for centuries have men of dominance changed the maps of the world, with armies and the sword.

But within the memory of men who live to-day another kind of empire-builder gave to the new world an empire of another kind. With peace and prosperity, year by year, he developed its vast square miles of territory. With rails of steel he pushed its boundaries each year still further into the wilderness. Each year he opened up to the world new acres of fertile fields, rich mines, and the tremendous natural resources of a virgin country. It is an empire that time can never destroy. It is an empire that has brought prosperity to the world.

All this was done by a poor Canadian boy, born in a log-cabin at the edge of the forest in the Province of Ontario, in the year 1837. James Jerome Hill was his name.

Jas. J. Hill

On his mother's side the boy inherited the sturdy characteristics of Scotch ancestry; on his father's side he found the brilliance and spirit of the Irish race. The soil was the sole source of their livelihood. Born in a wilderness where dark forests still sheltered wolves and deer, and where the Indians still roamed, the boy, from earliest childhood, received impressions that moulded his life's destiny. He was born to see man subdue the wilderness, to see his struggle with the forces of primitive nature, to see his inevitable victory. As his own father hewed his few acres from the forest, so in the coming years was James J. Hill to redeem vast wilderness territories and give them to the use of man.

Characteristically, the father's foresight sought more than an ordinary frontier education for his eldest son; and with equal eagerness the boy grasped at the opportunities that were offered him. At eleven he left the little district school where his education had begun, and entered an academy in a near-by village, conducted by an Englishman of college education.

There were no libraries, and in that remote outskirt of civilization newspapers were rarely seen. But a few books in the Hill household gave the growing boy an insight into literature, and the long hours of out-of-door labor which filled that part of the day when he was not at school developed him physically and gave him a foundation of good health which in later years made possible his tireless energy.

When he was fourteen his father died, and realizing the responsibilities which were now resting on his shoulders, the boy gave up his hope of a professional career and for four years supported his mother and her household with such small wages as he earned as clerk in the village store.

For several years, in the imaginative brain of the boy had grown the hope of some day crossing the Western plain and sailing across the Pacific to the Orient. Eagerly he had read all he could find that told him of those far countries. To his imagination they seemed to hold a definite promise of opportunity. He had but little money; but he had faith in himself and in his future. Each year the longing grew until, when he was eighteen, he could stand it no more and his new life began.

Without money, friends, or influence, he crossed the boundary into the United States, and after visiting several of the large Eastern cities, made his way to St. Paul, then a small town situated at the head of navigable water on the Mississippi River. North and west the unbroken prairie and the forests were peopled only by the Indians; buffalo roamed the prairies. Only along the navigable rivers were the cultivated farm-lands of the settlers.

The young man had no money; it was necessary for him to devote himself for a time to some profitable occupation. He was eighteen years old, but he was willing to turn his hand to any honest work, and his vivid imagination inspired him to work hard so that his future hopes might be realized. All of the business activity of St. Paul centred on the levees along the river, where merchandise brought up the Mississippi by boat was unloaded for shipment by ox-teams to the outlying settlements.

Hill was attracted by this kind of business. The position of shipping clerk in the office of the agents of a steamboat company was open, and he grasped it. The work was varied: he received incoming and outgoing freight, ran the warehouse, inspected its contents, kept an open eye for new business, and when labor was scarce, helped the men load and unload the steamboats. On this early experience was to be built the great triumph of coming years.

Not content with performing well his daily work, young Hill spent his evenings largely in studying the more technical and theoretical aspects of the transportation business and the possibilities, dependent upon adequate transportation, of the development of the great unexplored Northwest. Moreover, he saved his money, realizing that a time would come when his savings, however small, might prove vital to the grasping of an opportunity.

The year 1864 marks the close of the second period of his education. The great Civil War had torn the country. Hill, eager to serve his adopted land, had tried to enlist; but an accident in childhood which had resulted in the loss of an eye made it impossible to pass the physical examination. Although just beyond his majority, the boy had become a man in more than years. His steady attention to his work and the long hours of study had put him into a position from which he could now step fearlessly forward. He was a man of affairs.

The practical business knowledge and the business relationships which he had formed made him desire to be more completely his own master. It was not that he was tired of clerking; it was rather that he realized that the time had come to strike out for himself. To this resolve his young wife, Mary Theresa Mehegan, whom he had married in 1864, lent all her power of love and encouragement. A true partner in all her husband's plans, Mrs. Hill shared every struggle along the path of success.

The young business man became interested in many things. Far to the north was the great Red River country, and he began to identify himself with the traffic which was carried on between this territory and St. Paul. He developed his warehouse business; he became a dealer in salt, coal, cement, and lime; he transferred freight, and, above all, he studied the developments of railroading, with a realization that in the freight-car and the locomotive was the secret of the transportation of the future. Fuel particularly interested him, for he believed that, as the railroad train would supersede the steamboat, so would coal supplant wood as a motive power.

A year after resigning his clerkship, he entered into the first of the many partnerships which he formed during his life. His savings were now an asset of real value, and the $2500 which he had put by made the partnership possible. The partners planned to do a general transportation, commission, and storage business, and in 1866 he began his enlarged activities.

The following year Hill secured a contract with the

St. Paul and Pacific Railroad Company to supply it with fuel. It was his first real introduction to the railroad business, and on it were based the labors and successes of the coming years. The railroad in the Northwest was still in its infancy; transportation depended largely on the rivers and lakes.

During the next few years, Hill studied the transportation problems of the Northwest with constantly increasing faith in his belief that, by means of adequate transportation, it was possible speedily to develop this vast region for the use of man. More and more the idea appealed to him. His romantic vision led him on in his thoughts far beyond the boundaries which surrounded the mental vision of his fellow citizens, and his years of study and varied business experience enabled him, step by step, to turn his dreams into realities.

Steadily the railroads had extended westward from the Great Lakes. The end of the Mississippi River transportation was within sight. But from St. Paul to the rich lands of the Red River only the clumsy carts and the lake flatboats carried the merchandise which the settlers required. Present needs of adequate transportation were great; future requirements were enormous beyond comprehension. Hill went into the problem, and soon had a regular line of boats, carts, and steamers operating between St. Paul and Winnipeg. The empire-maker had begun to build.

Many are the stories that are told of Mr. Hill in those early days. In the heat of summer and in the blizzards of the northern winters he personally inspected and carried forward the work which he had designed. He endured every kind of hardship. On his steamboats in the open months, and with sled and dog train in winter, he passed back and forth over the route, examining every local condition, studying the soil, the climate, and the mineral deposits along the way.

On one late winter trip, when the bitter winds were sweeping across the snowy prairies, blotting out every landmark and turning the country into a vast white sea, he started north with dogs and sleds, and an Indian guide for a companion. After a few days the nerve of the Indian began to weaken and he urged that they turn back. Realizing that unless decided action was promptly taken the Indian might be dangerous, Hill ordered him to return, and set out again alone, camping by night among the snow-drifts, making tea with melted snow, and sleeping wrapped in his blankets, with his dogs close about him.

The first railroad actually to be constructed into this new territory was the St. Paul and Pacific. It received its charter in 1858, under the name of the Minnesota & Pacific Railroad Company, and was planned to extend from Stillwater, through St. Paul and Minneapolis, west to Breckenridge. Immediately a craze for railroads swept the Northwest, and numbers of companies were formed; but such frenzied speculation could end only in disaster, and one by one the companies fell into bankruptcy.

With anxious eyes Hill watched the rising and waning fortunes of these various railroad enterprises.

His investigation led him to believe that the St. Paul & Pacific offered the greatest possibilities. For seventeen long years he worked hard, dreamed his dreams, and added to his capital. Then came the opportunity. The St. Paul & Pacific had become a wrecked property. In it he saw the possibilities for which he had worked and saved. With a clear realization of the tremendous step that he was taking, he cast his entire fortune into the balance, and with the assistance of several associates took over the property, and with it its enormous debt of over $33,000,000. James J. Hill at last held control of a railroad.

He had bought a property that was bankrupt and was described as "two streaks of rust reaching out into the desert"; but in this bold beginning was the germ of the great railroad system which, under the name of the Great Northern, was to bring him fame and fortune in the years to come.

In the six years that followed, Mr. Hill extended his railroad to the Red River and connected with the government line from Winnipeg. By this extension the rich lands of Minnesota were opened to immigrants, and the great wheat-lands of the Northwest were connected with the markets of the United States.

The risk that he had taken was justified; but to his wife and to the friends who knew him it seemed less great, for they knew the character of the man, and to know him was to feel complete confidence in any action which he determined to take. "All his life it was his custom to know all the facts about anything in which he was interested, a good deal earlier and a little better than anybody else. For twenty years he had lived in the country where the situation had been preparing. For four or five years he had been consumed with anxiety to get possession of this property. He alone fully understood its present value; he alone conceived its future with any degree of justness."

But now his dreams of a greater empire began to be realized. The St. Paul & Pacific, under his able management, was earning money and building up a surplus. In 1883 Mr. Hill extended it to Helena, Montana. And now his belief in the development of the Northwest was more strongly confirmed with each new step. His vision already pictured a railroad stretching across the prairies and over the tremendous barrier of the Rocky Mountains to the Pacific and the great harbors of Puget Sound. This was no impractical dream, but an idea founded on fact and experience; it was a great constructive enterprise.

Ten years later, in 1893, Mr. Hill began actively to carry out his plan of extending his railroad from Helena to the coast. It is hard to realize the tremendous difficulties which faced him. On the one hand, the Rocky Mountains seemed to block his path; on the other, a financial panic made the obtaining of the money necessary for the project seem almost an impossibility. But he was undismayed; every obstacle was overcome, the road was built, and the empire again extended its boundary, this time to the blue waters of the Pacific.

Following the completion of the Great Northern, as the consolidation of his various railroads was now

called, to Puget Sound, Mr. Hill began his struggle to
obtain the control of other railroads in order to com-
bine them all into one vast coherent system. The
Northern Pacific Railroad was the first to be added,
and then the Burlington System was secured and in-
corporated into the vast development of his plan.
Fifty years before, the penniless country boy had left
the small village of his birth to seek his fortune; and
now, after this life of usefulness, he found himself able
to pay in cash over $200,000,000 for the Northern
Pacific Railway System.

Mr. Hill believed that the tilling of the soil was the
true basis of success; that on the soil rested the stabil-
ity of government, and that from it came the wealth
of the world. To him, his vast systems of railroads
were the means of opening to settlement regions of
arable land, and later, when these lands had been cultivated, of connecting them with the rest of the world
and affording markets for their produce. To increase
population and industry along a railroad was the sur-
est way of making the railroad profitable. He believed that a railroad would be rich or poor along with
the farmers who cultivated the fields beside its tracks.

In order to help the thousands of farmers along the
lines of his railroads to make their farms more profitable, Mr. Hill bought, wherever in the world they
could be best obtained, herds of the finest cattle.
These he bred on his own farms, and many he gave
away to the farmers for their own breeding. In all, he
gave away more than eight thousand head of cattle
and hogs, and for many years offered prizes for the

9

best cattle raised by the farmers. "We must have better farming," he said. "We must have more intelligent methods. Experience has shown that there is no way in which they can do this so well as by raising cattle, pigs, and horses, and by dairying."

As a boy he had dreamed of the Orient. Now his dreams were to be realized. From the Western states his trains came eastward heavily loaded with lumber from the great forests of Oregon and Washington. To operate most profitably, it was apparent that these trains should not go west empty, but filled with merchandise. But there were not enough people in these Western states to consume the merchandise the trains could carry. Beyond the Pacific, however, were millions of people. China and Japan needed many things. Why should not his railroads carry westward merchandise for these great markets of the Orient?

With characteristic thoroughness, Mr. Hill sent agents to China to study the food-problem, and the best way to make a market there for American flour. They reported the existence of a great market for flour, cotton, and steel. To gain this business was to wage industrial warfare with Belgium and Great Britain, who had a cheap all-water route to the Orient by way of the Suez Canal.

But as his railroads extended only to the Pacific shore, a great ocean still lay between him and these alluring markets. To solve this problem, Mr. Hill formed, in 1900, the Great Northern Steamship Company, and built the Minnesota and the Dakota, the greatest vessels ever built flying the American flag, to run between Seattle and Yokohama and Hong Kong. But in this great venture, with its promise of success, Mr. Hill encountered disappointment, for the policy of the United States was unfavorable, rates and regulations made the cost of the operation of the ships excessive, and he was at last forced by circumstances to withdraw from the Oriental field.

Meanwhile, the vast empire of the Northwest was rapidly filling up with settlers. In a single year eighteen thousand farmers located along the Great Northern, and each year, farther and farther back from the tracks, new lands were developed and new homes were located where only a few years before the buffalo and the Indians had wandered. Next after the railroad, it was the farm which held the closest interest of the empire-builder.

Second only to Mr. Hill's belief in the farm as the foundation of national prosperity was his interest in the discovery and development of new sources of mineral wealth. As a young man he had recognized the tremendous part which coal was to play in the history of transportation and the consequent development of the country. For years he had studied the coal deposits of the Northwest, and there was probably no one better informed than he regarding their quality, extent, and location.

In like manner he had investigated the general facts regarding the world's supply of iron ore. At this time, however, there were no known deposits of iron ore in the Northwest. Then came rumors of the discovery of iron deposits in northern Minnesota. But now Mr.

Hill's two oldest sons were taking an active interest in the vast operations of their father. Like him, they had traveled extensively, not only over the territory reached by his railroads, but also over the still undeveloped lands, particularly in northern Minnesota.

In this way the two younger men became convinced of the wealth of iron ore which awaited only proper development and railroad connections to yield an enormous profit. Mr. Hill saw also the great opportunity that presented itself, and in 1899 personally purchased, for $4,050,000, a great tract of land on the now famous Mesabi Range. Immediately, railroad connections with the iron country were constructed, and arrangements for the shipment of the ore over the Great Northern were made. But although this was in every respect a private venture, practically discovered and entirely paid for by Mr. Hill out of his own pocket, his high sense of honor and responsibility refused to accept the enormous profits which were soon to be realized. Believing that the stockholders of the Great Northern, who with their money had stood behind him and had in a measure made this new development possible, were entitled to a share in the profits, he organized this new mining project, and distributed its stock, share for share, among them in proportion to their investment in the railroad. His refusal to take the entire profit is a fine example of the high principles which guided his every act and were in large measure responsible for his success.

Throughout his life, Mr. Hill believed that the success of men and nations rests entirely on the truest personal liberty. To him the man was always bigger than the state. Personal initiative and effort came first; what man individually could not accomplish, that the state must do; but never should the state assume the development or operation of a project until it was recognized that an individual or a group of individuals could not better accomplish the desired result.

The forest, the farm, and the mines, were in his belief the three sources of wealth. But wealth could come only from universal industry, honesty, thrift, and fair dealing among men. In his own dealings with his fellow men, he required those qualities; and, although his keen sympathies invariably responded to true distress, he had scant patience with those whose false vision saw in wealth honestly acquired a fund to be drawn upon for the support of the lazy and shiftless.

He once said: "There are four great words that should be written upon the four corner-stones of every public building in the country, with the sacredness of a religious rite. These watchwards of the Republic are Equality, Simplicity, Economy, and Justice." And another time he said, when speaking of a profit-sharing arrangement he had made with his employees: "I am as well satisfied with that institution as with anything I have ever had to do with. I think that its greatest value is teaching the men to save. The first two or three hundred dollars is the hardest to save, but when once you have started, you all know it comes easy."

Long before his death Mr. Hill's name had become known throughout the civilized world. "His fame was international.   His services were cosmopolitan." Among the many honors which were heaped upon him in recognition of his services to mankind was the degree of Doctor of Laws by Yale University.   In conferring this degree, Professor Perrin, of Yale, said: —

"Mr. Hill is the last of the generations of wilderness conquerors, the men who interpreted the Constitution, fixed our foreign relations, framed the Monroe Doctrine, and blazed all the great trails which determined the nation's future.   He has always been an original investigator, and we know him now as a man of infinite information.   Every item of his colossal success rests upon a series of facts ascertained by him before they had been noted by others, and upon the future relations which he saw in those facts to human need and national growth.   He believes that no society can prosper in which intellectual training is not based upon moral and religious culture.   He is a national economist on broad ethical and religious lines; but the greatest things in all his greatness are his belief in the spiritual significance of man and his longing for the perpetuation of American institutions at their highest and best."

His interest in books as a source of education found expression in the great public library which he presented to the city of St. Paul.   To him, the trained mind was a necessity for success.   Whether trained in the university or in the active life of the world did not matter, so long as it was trained; that was all that concerned him.

Mr. Hill's reputation in years to come will rest chiefly on his career as an "Empire-Builder." But he was primarily a railroad manager and a railroad engineer. His knowledge of the great business of transportation made it possible for him to extend his interests far and wide; no opportunity came near him that he did not investigate, and no opportunity which he accepted was ever put aside until he had developed it to its most perfect completion.

Physically, he was a man who seemed to express in his appearance the force and character which distinguished him mentally among men. Slightly under average height, with a great head firmly set on square, powerful shoulders, he commanded attention. He was physically strong, and his powers of endurance, which served him so well in the long hard days of his early life, remained unimpaired almost to his death. His firm mouth was half hidden by a beard, whitened in his latter years. His brow was high. His eyes were alert and looked out from beneath shaggy eyebrows. He was a man of a notable appearance which demanded respect and inspired confidence.

"Work, hard work, intelligent work, and then some more work," was one of his frequent explanations of his success, and his advice to others. To young men he said: "The best advice to a young man, as it appears to me, is old and simple. Get knowledge and understanding. Determine to make the most possible of yourself by doing to the best of your power useful work as it comes your way. There are no receipts for success in life. A good aim, diligence in learning every detail of your business, honest hard work, and a determination to succeed, win out every time, unless crossed by some exceptional accident or misfortune. Many opportunities come to every man. It depends upon himself, and upon what he shall make of himself, what he makes of opportunities and what they will make of him."

From a poor farmer boy, in fifty years, James J. Hill, by the force of his own determination, and the opportunities common to all men in the great Republic of which he became a citizen, achieved a position among the world-leaders of his day. Wealth in millions came to him, not by inheritance or a stroke of speculative chance, but from the works which he himself had conceived and created. The achievements of his life will long be remembered, not only because of their public service, but because of their inspiration to other men by affording an example of the heights which may be reached by hard work, imagination, and determination to succeed.

VIII

AUGUSTUS SAINT-GAUDENS

Born in Dublin, Ireland, 1848
Died in Cornish, New Hampshire, 1907

In a little house in Dublin, Ireland, on March 1, 1848, was born Augustus Saint-Gaudens. There was nothing in the humble surroundings which first greeted his eyes to mark the baby as in any way different from the many other babies who may have been born on the same first day of March in the ancient Irish city.

Augustus Saint-Gaudens, however, inherited from his father and mother something far greater than wealth or name, for in their sturdy, honest blood he found that indefinable thing called "character," which, throughout his life, led him steadily forward along the straight path to fame and honor. From his parents he also inherited the qualities which are inherent in a romantic people; for his father was born in France, in the little village of Aspet at the foot of the Pyrenees, and his mother, whose maiden name was Mary McGuiness, gave him the love of the beautiful which belongs to Ireland. But perhaps, after all, his parents gave him a like inheritance, for Ireland is an old nation into which in centuries past has been infused the blood of the proudest families of France — Irish by birth and French by inheritance, he might be called.

The elder Saint-Gaudens was a shoemaker, and he had met the mother of the future Augustus in the shoe store for which he made shoes and where she did the binding of slippers. When Augustus was but a few months old his parents emigrated to the United States and in the month of September in the year of his birth he landed in the city of Boston, a place which in later years became deeply identified with his activities.

From Boston the little family proceeded to New York, where Bernard Saint-Gaudens, the father, set up his small business and secured humble lodging nearby for his family. And here the young Augustus made the beginning of his conscious life, in which, of early memories, most vivid were the "delightful reminiscences of the smell of cake in the bakery at the corner of the street, and of the stewed peaches of the German family in the same house."

Above the door of the shop hung the sign "French Ladies' Boots and Shoes"; and within, the shoemaker, with his "wonderfully complex mixture of French accent and Irish brogue" varied his occupation of making shoes with endless duties which he undertook as the organizer and leading figure in several societies which flourished in the French colony of the city. Customers came readily to the little shop, for its proprietor was an able workman, despite certain agreeable eccentricities, and the business, growing steadily, provided an adequate, if simple, upbringing for Augustus and his two brothers.

Many are the memories of those early days, mem-

Copyright, 1915, by de W. C. Ward

ories of a wholesome and normal boyhood. There are memories of fires, of street-fights with boys of other neighborhoods, of school-days, of a never-to-be-forgotten excursion to the country, of the delight of his first reading of " Robinson Crusoe," and of the famous actress Rachel playing "Virginia" in Niblo's Garden. And there are memories of boyhood loves, memories all that "pass across the field of my vision like ships that appear through the mist for a moment and disappear."

With the early end of his school days Augustus turned to the actual earning of his daily bread. He was thirteen years old. To his father's question as to what kind of work appealed most strongly to him he had answered, "I should like it if I could do something which would help me to be an artist." It was a decision that must have seemed strange to the father, who perhaps had seen in the boy a possible assistant in his growing business; but wisely he respected the desire that Augustus expressed, and a few weeks later the boy was apprenticed to a Frenchman named Avet, the first stone-cameo cutter in America.

A cameo is a fine relief of a human head, or the head of an animal, cut in a stone or shell, often so done as to show the design in a layer of one color with another color as a background. The stones, which were usually amethysts or malachite, were at that period extremely fashionable, and were worn in rings, or scarf-pins, or breast-pins by men and women. The work was fine and required skill and patience and artistic ability; so for a long time Augustus was limited to the preparation of the stones, which Avet would finish and later sell to the leading jewelers of the city.

Avet was a hard taskmaster and the monotonous labor over the whirring lathe was irksome to the red-blooded boy, who looked up from the spinning-wheel at the white clouds sailing across the little window above him and heard the rumble of wheels and the hum of life in the distant street. But in his few hours of leisure there were glimpses of stirring events never to be forgotten. There was the excitement attending the election of Abraham Lincoln to the Presidency, "Honest Abe, the Rail-Splitter." There was the recruiting of troops for the great Civil War which for four long years racked the land. And later, from the window in front of his lathe, Saint-Gaudens watched the volunteers from New England as they tramped down Broadway, singing "John Brown's Body" as they marched.

Day after day Saint-Gaudens ground and turned the stones on his lathe, and all day long he listened to the voice of Avet, scolding and swearing as he worked. One day came the breaking-point. At noon the boy had quietly eaten his luncheon from the little box which he brought each morning with him to his work. Some crumbs had fallen on the floor, and Avet, seeing them, burst into a fury and discharged him on the spot. Without comment he folded up his overalls, left the shop, and going at once to his father's store, explained exactly what had occurred. Within a few minutes Avet followed, apologetic and promising even more money if the boy would return. Without hesitation Saint-Gaudens refused, and in later life he often recalled his father's "proud smile" as he made his decision

There is credit in sticking to a hard job, and there is equal credit in a manly refusal to continue to work under intolerable conditions. Saint-Gaudens's act brought its own reward, for his next employer, Mr. Jules le Brethon, a shell-cameo cutter, was a man unlike Avet in every particular, and it was through this new connection that the path to Saint-Gaudens's career as a sculptor was opened to him.

With his characteristic foresight in availing himself of every opportunity, the boy had early begun to devote his evenings to the study of drawing in the free classes at the Cooper Institute. Every day at six he left his work, and after a hurried supper, hastened to his classroom. He was appreciative of the great opportunity which the school afforded him, and he threw himself with all his soul into his work. "I became a terrific worker, toiling every night until eleven o'clock after the class was over. Indeed, I became so exhausted with the confining work of cameo-cutting by day and drawing at night, that in the morning mother literally dragged me out of bed, pushed me over to the washstand, where I gave myself a cat's lick somehow or other, drove me to the seat at the table, administered my breakfast, and tumbled me downstairs out into the street, where I awoke."

When the courses at the Cooper Union were finally accomplished, Saint-Gaudens took up new night work at the National Academy of Design, and it was here that his first appreciation of the antique came to him, and his first practice in drawing from the nude — training so fundamental for his great work in coming years.

Early in the year 1867 came another turning-point in his life. Ever since he had first begun to work, Saint-Gaudens had been giving his wages to his father to pay his share of the family expenses. And now the father, realising that the boy's earnestness and ability were deserving of every opportunity which he could afford, made the offer of a trip to Europe, where he might see the art of the older civilizations and return to the United States broadened by his experience and observations.

Saint-Gaudens was nineteen years old. His father had paid for his passage in the steerage, and in his pocket were a hundred dollars which had been saved out of his wages. Arriving in Paris in a "mixed state of enthusiasm and collapse," he spent a few days visiting in the household of an uncle, and then began his search of employment at cameo-cutting and of admission to the School of Fine Arts. Work was soon found in the establishment of an Italian. But entrance to the school was a more difficult proposition, and in order that no time should be wasted while he was waiting, he enrolled in a modeling school, working there mornings and nights and supporting himself on what he earned at cameo-cutting in the afternoon.

These were days and nights of almost superhuman exertion, but at the end of a year the desired admission to the school was obtained, and his real education began. It is customary for a student at the Beaux-Arts to select the master in whose atelier he wishes to study, and Saint-Gaudens selected Jouffroy, whose pupils in the preceding years had been particularly successful in capturing most of the prizes which were offered by the school.

Here Saint-Gaudens formed several friendships which endured throughout his life, and here also he began to mingle more widely with the men in the great world about him, although his time was far too occupied for more than an occasional hour or two of relaxation. "My ambition was of such a soaring nature, and I was so tremendously austere, that I had the deepest scorn of the ordinary amusements of the light opera, balls and what not." And yet, when he did play, his play was of the hardest. He was active beyond measure, and it is doubtless to the hours of hard physical exercise which he got at night in the gymnasium and the swimming-baths, that he owed the health which gave him the endurance necessary for his long hours in the classroom. Occasionally, walking trips, with one or two companions, gave well-deserved vacations — trips from which the walkers returned tired and penniless, but inspired by the beauty of nature in the pleasant French countryside and thrilled with the stupendous grandeur of the Alpine scenery.

But now, in the year 1870, the dark clouds of the Franco-Prussian War suddenly gathered. War was declared. The streets of Paris were congested with shouting, marching crowds. The enlistment places were filled with men joining the colors. To the young American the problem of his own line of action seemed difficult to decide. Everything within him urged him to enlist under the flag of France. But he was a citizen of another land, and aged parents awaited his return. He decided to withhold his decision. Once, indeed, he returned to Paris from Limoges fixed in his purpose to join his French companions; but there he found a letter from his mother, so pathetic that he reluctantly abandoned his intention, returned to Limoges, and a few months later started for Rome.

After the cold, gray months of a Paris winter, and the misery and suffering of the war, the glowing warmth and beauty of the Holy City exhilarated and exalted him. "It was as if a door had been thrown wide open to the eternal beauty of the classical." Here, living almost in poverty, he continued the work so well begun in Paris. Here, also, he began the statue of Hiawatha, "pondering, musing in the forest, on the welfare of his people"— the first of the long list of world-recognized masterpieces which the strenuous labor of his life produced. So poor, indeed, was Saint-Gaudens at this time, that it was only through the kindness of an American, who advanced him the money to cast the figure, that he was able to complete the work. For this same gentleman Saint-Gaudens modeled busts of his two daughters, and through him he also received a commission for copies of the busts of Demosthenes and Cicero.

In Rome Saint-Gaudens also first made the acquaintance of Dr. Henry Shiff, a comrade whose friendship lasted throughout his life. Shiff was considerably the senior of Saint-Gaudens, but his deep appreciation of art and literature, and his frank, friendly nature endeared him to the young and struggling sculptor, and gave him the inspiration that is always found in the true appreciation of a loyal friend.

In 1872 Saint-Gaudens returned to New York; but his stay was brief, for he was eager to return to Italy for a few years more before definitely establishing himself in the United States. While in New York, much work was accomplished, but little of it should be included in a list of his works, for in the main it consisted of jobs of one sort or another necessary to earn the money which his living required. Here, however, he began his bust of Senator William M. Evarts, one of the foremost orators in the United States, and, during the years 1877 to 1881, Secretary of State in the administration of President Hayes. Then, also, he received a number of other commissions for busts and, of particular importance, a commission for a figure of Silence to be placed in a Masonic building in New York. It was a sudden and bewildering amount of work for the young sculptor, and it brought vividly to him, after his struggling years of poverty in Europe, a realization of the appreciation and reward which the United States so freely offered.

In 1875 Augustus Saint-Gaudens returned again to the United States, but this time to take his place as a full-fledged sculptor. Behind him were years of hard but fruitful experience. From the long period at which he had worked at his cameo-cutting he had developed a keen eye and a sure hand with his tools. From Paris and Rome he had obtained the practice which he required in actual work from the human figure, and from Rome in particular he had learned "what to leave untouched" and had acquired "an ability to choose his subjects from among the important figures of the moment, and then to give his best efforts to transforming them into vital and eternal symbols."

On his arrival in New York he rented a small studio in an old building, and was soon intensively occupied in a life in which modeling, teaching, and studying filled the long hours, and carried on often far into the night. Dark and depressing seemed the New York winter after the warmth and color of Italy; and to bring back more vividly the memory of the tinkling, splashing fountains that played in the Roman sunshine, he would turn on the water in the little wash-basin in his studio and let the gentle sound carry his thoughts back to the gardens of Rome.

But now came two commissions which left no opportunity for thoughts of anything but the work in hand. From Governor Dix of New York came a commission for a statue of Robert Richard Randall, a wealthy citizen of New York City in the early years of the nineteenth century, who had left his fortune for the founding of the Sailors' Snug Harbor, on Staten Island, a home for aged deep-sea sailormen. At the same time he obtained a commission for the statue of Admiral David G. Farragut, — the first Admiral of the United States Navy, and the hero of Mobile Bay,

— which stands in Madison Square, New York. The importance of these commissions did much to raise the spirits and fire the ambition of Saint-Gaudens, and at the same time the constantly increasing friendships which he was forming helped him to find the happiness of congenial comradeship which his nature sought. "There is no doubt," he has written, "that my intimacy with John LaFarge has been a spur to higher endeavor"; and there were others who gave him similar inspiration by their warm appreciation of his ambitions.

It was in the year 1877 that Saint-Gaudens took a principal part in the founding of the Society of American Artists. The establishment of this society was an important milestone in the progress of American art, for with it came a vital change in American painting and sculpture. Previously, art in the United States had been more or less burdened with conventions and a dull technique. But this stagnant state now became stirred and freshened by the flood of a new generation of artists. Such men as Saint-Gaudens, Eastman Johnson, John LaFarge, Winslow Homer, and John S. Sargent began to remonstrate against the things that were. These men and their fellows had felt abroad the new movement in artistic appreciation. It was their desire to give to America this new and virile expression, and in spite of the opposition of the conservatists of the established school, — the "old-timers,"— the new society received a welcome and became a constantly increasing factor and force in the development of American art.

A year was now spent in the modeling of a high bas-relief depicting the "Adoration of the Cross by Angels," which was to form the principal part of the interior decorations of St. Thomas's Church in New York, which were being designed by Mr. John LaFarge. This was important work and added greatly to Saint-Gaudens's reputation; but only the memory of its beauty remains, for the church was later destroyed by fire.

In 1878 Saint-Gaudens again visited Paris, but this time his work and study held him there for three years. In a quiet studio which he hired in the Rue Notre Dame des Champs, work was begun on the Farragut statue, and also on a series of figures which were designed to ornament a mausoleum which Governor Morgan of Connecticut had commissioned him to execute. It is a strange coincidence that the angels for the Morgan tomb were later destroyed by fire, as were the angels of St. Thomas's Church.

"In the years I passed this time in Paris there was little of the adventurous swing of life that pervaded my previous struggles." Work on his commissions almost wholly occupied him. There were, however, occasional excursions, and the presence of two friends, Stanford White and McKim, who were already winning their reputation as brilliant New York architects, did much to break the tedium of his work.

The Farragut statue was finally completed, and on the afternoon of a beautiful day in May, 1881, it was unveiled to the eyes of the public. In his "Reminiscences" Saint-Gaudens described this memorable occasion: "These formal unveilings of monuments are impressive affairs and variations from the toughness that pervades a sculptor's life. For we constantly deal with practical problems, with moulders, contractors, derricks, stone-men, ropes, builders, scaffoldings, marble assistants, bronze-men, trucks, rubbish-men, plasterers, and what-not else, all the while trying to soar into the blue. — But if managed intelligently there is a swing to unveilings, and the moment when the veil drops from the monument certainly makes up for many of the woes that go towards the creating of the work. On this special occasion Mr. Joseph H. Choate delivered the oration. The sailors who assisted added to the picturesqueness of the procession. The artillery placed in the park, back of the statue, was discharged. And when the figure in the shadow stood unveiled, and the smoke rolled up into the sunlight upon the buildings behind it, the sight gave an impression of dignity and beauty that it would take a rare pen to describe."

During the year 1877 Saint-Gaudens was married to Augusta F. Homer of Boston. Recognition had come to his work; his professional future seemed assured. Now, by this happy marriage, domestic tranquillity and congenial companionship were added.

On his return from Europe Saint-Gaudens took a studio on Thirty-Sixth Street in New York, and here were begun the Sunday afternoon concerts which soon became celebrated because of the literary men and artists who gathered there, and invitations were eagerly sought and highly prized. But in 1885 Saint-Gaudens moved from the city and established his family in an old Colonial house at Cornish, New Hampshire. "I had been a boy of the streets and sidewalks all my life," he says, "but during this first summer in the country, it dawned on me seriously how much there was outside of my little world." Here was open country, a land of green hills and sky, a place where the man to whom beauty was a living thing might find widening inspiration.

Of the many monuments which Saint-Gaudens created there are five which commemorate great heroes of the Civil War. The monument of Admiral Farragut has been mentioned; standing in the heart of the country's greatest city, it carries daily to the thousands who pass an unconscious inspiration — as though treading the swinging deck of his flagship, the Admiral seems to look forward with a grim determination, inflexible, indomitable — a man.

The Shaw memorial was undertaken in 1884. The second of this historic series, Saint-Gaudens expected to complete it within a comparatively short time; but it was not until 1897 that the memorial was unveiled in Boston. Robert Gould Shaw was a young Bostonian who was killed in action while leading his regiment, the Fifty-fourth Massachusetts — a regiment of colored men led by white officers. The memorial is in the form of a large bas-relief. Although unfortunately placed, it is one of Saint-Gaudens's most highly considered works. Across the relief the colored troops march to the drum beat; there is the rhythm of a passing regiment and a martial animation, but over all is a sense of melancholy; in the faces of the soldiers, the tense look of anticipation of the impending battle. Occupying the centre of the panel, Shaw rides beside his men, an expression of sadness on his youthful face. Above the scene floats a figure to which the master gave no name, but which his interpreters and pupils have called Fame and Death.

During the early nineties Saint-Gaudens produced two more statues, both of which have been placed in the city of Chicago. In the equestrian monument to General Logan, Saint-Gaudens gave an indication of the greater statue, that of General Sherman, which was soon to follow. In the Logan monument he found a subject susceptible of broad interpretation. The general, mounted on a spirited charger, rides with the air of a conqueror. There is the "smell of the battlefield" in his face. The body seems a living thing, moving flesh and blood are incased in the wind-blown uniform.

But in his statue of Abraham Lincoln, Saint-Gaudens reached the height of his art. Standing before the massive chair from which he seems to have risen, the tall, gaunt, ungainly figure embodies in its attitude and in every hanging fold of the unfitted garments, the spirit of infinite tenderness, melancholy, and strength that characterized the great emancipator. Although the memory of Lincoln will endure as long as men live upon the earth, the Lincoln of Saint-Gaudens will ever recall to coming generations the plaintive sadness of this greatest of Americans.

In the year 1887 General William Tecumseh Sherman gave Saint-Gaudens eighteen sittings for a bust. Sherman had served with distinction in the Mexican War in 1846, and in May, 1861, at the outbreak of the Civil War, was appointed colonel of the Thirteenth U.S. Infantry. Rapidly promoted, he took part in many famous campaigns, and in 1864 became commander of the military division of the Mississippi. Assembling in 1864 his three armies, comprising over one hundred thousand men, near Chattanooga, he began an invasion of the State of Georgia, and finally, with 60,000 picked men, made his celebrated "March to the Sea," from Atlanta to Savannah. The statue of Sherman was begun in 1890, but it was not until 1903 that it was finally erected at the entrance of Central Park in New York City. Led by a symbolic figure of Victory, the general rides forward on his charger. A speaking likeness of Sherman, the statue at the same time seems infused with the spirit of the great struggle, a spirit of invincible determination. It is a monument which may be included among the great equestrian statues of the modern world. "His horse is obviously advancing, and Sherman's body, tense with nervous energy, is at one with the body beneath him, equally impressive of movement. The winged victory in every fibre quivers with the rhythm of oncoming resistless force."

In the Rock Creek Cemetery near the City of Washington is a figure which is not only one of the greatest productions of Saint-Gaudens, but unquestionably his most imaginative composition. This is the memorial erected by Mr. Henry Adams to his wife. The figure is seated and concealed by a loose garment which half veils the face. Saint-Gaudens once spoke of the figure as symbolic of "The Mystery of the Hereafter; it is beyond pain, and beyond joy." Of this monument Henry Adams wrote to Saint-Gaudens: "The work is indescribably noble and imposing . . . it is full of poetry and suggestion, infinite wisdom, a past without beginning and a future without end, a repose after limitless experience, a peace to which nothing matters — all are embodied in this austere and beautiful face and form."

The world now began to pour its offerings upon Saint-Gaudens. From Harvard University came the honorary degree of LL.D. and the tribute of Dr. Eliot, its president, who said in conferring it: "Augustus Saint-Gaudens — sculptor whose art follows but ennobles nature, confers fame and lasting remembrance, and does not count the mortal years it takes to mould immortal forms." Degrees from the Universities of Yale and Princeton followed his Harvard honor; at Paris in 1900 he was awarded the medal of honor, "and at Buffalo in the following year a special medal was bestowed upon him, an enthusiastic tribute from his fellow artists, who sought lovingly to exalt him above themselves as the one man they regarded as the master of them all."

Together with these recognitions came others of equal significance. In the late nineties he was made by the French Government an Officer of the Legion of Honor and a Corresponding Member of the Société des Beaux-Arts, and later from the same source came an offer to purchase certain of his bronzes for the Luxembourg Museum in Paris. In 1904 he was elected Honorary Foreign Academician of the Royal Academy of London, and among his other later distinctions may be included his memberships in the National Academy of New York and the Academy of St. Luke, Rome.

Constantly he answered the call of Europe and found delight and profit in his travels; but the United States grew more dear to him with each passing year. "I belong in America," he wrote; "that is my home, that is where I want to be and to remain." But now the tireless energy of his early life began to show its mark on the vigorous vitality which had so long supported him. With his work, and congenial assistants and friends, he began to identify himself more closely with the simple life of his Cornish home. On the third of August, 1907, came the final episode in his memorable career. A long illness attended by much suffering had failed to separate him from his work; carried to his studio to superintend the work of his assistants, he labored until the end. But his life was over, and as he had lived in a realm of spiritual beauty, so in the quiet peace of the New Hampshire hills his spirit passed.

Augustus Saint-Gaudens, although of foreign birth and for many years, during the early period of his life, a resident abroad, "remained as distinctly American in his art as if he had come from a long line of native ancestors. He showed his Americanism in striking out in a totally new vein and making his own traditions."

Of his art much has been written, but a few quotations may suffice. "The special note of the medallions which are conspicuous among his first productions is one of delicacy, and in the character of that delicacy lies a source of strength which was from first to last of immense service." His touch was "at once caressing and bold," and he delighted "in giving a clear, even forcible, impression of the personality before him. It is portraiture for the sake of truth and beauty, not for the sake of technique." In his work in the round, the Adams memorial stands as his "one memorable effort in the sphere of loftiest abstraction. His other greatest triumphs were won in the field of portraiture." In his studies of historical subjects, Saint-Gaudens "struck the one definitive note, made his Lincoln or Sherman a type which generations must revere and which no future statues can invalidate."

"People think a sculptor has an easy life in a studio," he once said. "It's hard labor in a factory." And often he remarked, "You can do anything you please. It's the way it's done that makes the difference."

Such was Augustus Saint-Gaudens. To him America afforded an opportunity; richly and many times over did he repay his debt to his adopted land.

IX

JACOB A. RIIS

Born in Ribe, Denmark, 1849
Died in Barre, Massachusetts, 1914

THERE are many good citizens of the United States who can look back with pride to their Danish ancestry. Denmark, that land of low-lying, storm-swept coasts, and level plains, has bred for centuries a race of hardy, freedom-loving people. It is only natural that America should hold out to them a promise of even greater opportunity and personal liberty.

On the bleak coast of the North Sea is the little town of Ribe. There, in 1849, was born Jacob A. Riis, son of a schoolmaster and one of fourteen children. Scant were the means for the education and upbringing of so large a family; but from this humble home on the Danish seacoast came a man who, in later years, was to become famous in the new land of his adoption: famous, not because of wealth or inventive genius, but for his citizenship, and for his deeds, which left the world better than he found it.

There were no railroads or steamboats in Ribe in those days. It was as it had been almost for centuries. And yet Ribe took pride in its history: its people were a fighting race, fighters for honor and liberty, fighters for the little of peace and security that encroaching neighbors and unfriendly Nature had permitted them

to have. They had fought back the Germans in 1849, as they had fought for their homes in years before. And every year, when the wind set in from the north-west, they fought back the sea that rose up over the low beaches and flooded the land as far back as the eye could see.

With such traditions and in such environment, it is small wonder that young Jacob grew to be a healthy, normal boy charged with ambition and energy. There was fighting blood in his veins, but it was the blood that rises and fights against oppression and for the right, and never for conquest or the subjection of the weak.

It was the ambition of the father that Jacob should study for a professional career, but to the young boy, with his strong body and alert mind, the study of a trade appealed more keenly, and he was apprenticed for a year to a carpenter in the town.

But before the year was done, the boy's ambition grew beyond the opportunities of the little town, and, with the consent of his family, he removed to Copen-hagen to continue his apprenticeship under a great builder in that city. Four years were passed here, and during these years Jacob became proficient in his trade; but of even greater value were the opportuni-ties for study which the Danish capital afforded him: study not only in books, but in men and in the obser-vation of the life around him.

One other thing drove his ambition steadily for-ward. In Ribe was a fair-haired girl, the daughter of the wealthiest and most prominent citizen. Wide was the social and financial gulf between the young and penniless carpenter and the young girl whom he desired for his wife. To everyone but himself his hopes seemed almost ridiculous in their impossibility. He alone refused to accept defeat. If money was needed, he would make it. If Denmark could not offer him success, there was a land beyond the Atlantic that could.

He was twenty-one years old. In his pocket were forty dollars. It was not much, either in years of experience or in wealth; but he had his trade to fall back on, and, above all, he had "a pair of strong hands and stubbornness enough to do for two; also a strong belief that in a free country, free from the dominion of custom, of caste, as well as of men, things would somehow come right in the end."

From the deck of the steamer he watched the city of New York grow large on the horizon. Ships of the world filled the blue harbor. Tall spires of churches lifted above the roofs; wharves were alive with activity. A static quality was in the air; he was filled with a spirit of adventure and limitless opportunity.

In Castle Garden, at the tip of New York, where in years past the immigrants were landed, a man was hiring laborers in an iron-works at Brady's Bend in Pennsylvania. The pay seemed good, and Riis engaged to join the party which was being formed.

The work was hard, but Riis's knowledge of a trade stood him in good stead, and he was put at work building houses for the employees in the foundry. Then from a clear sky came news which abruptly changed his plans and the course of his entire life. France had declared war on Prussia, and Denmark was expected to join with France and avenge her wrongs of 1864.

Back to his memory came the love of his own country, of her flag, and of what seemed his duty there. His brain aflame with patriotism, he threw up his job and hurried to Buffalo, and from there proceeded finally to New York. He had just one cent in his pocket; he had sold his clothes and small possessions to buy his ticket.

But the Frenchmen in New York did not understand the young Dane who wanted them to send him home to fight if his country needed him; nor did those of his own countrymen whom he saw feel able to pay his transportation on this patriotic journey. Again and again young Riis offered himself. At every attempt rebuff or misfortune countered him. It was useless to try further. Reluctantly he abandoned his hope to join the French in their great struggle.

Winter was at hand. To the scantily clad, starving, and penniless young man, the great city seemed to turn a cold and forbidding shoulder. But opportunity does not come to those who wait expectant of it: it is a prize to be won by struggle, and often by privation. Opportunity is everywhere, but it is only the stalwart, indomitable spirits who seek and seize it.

Hard days followed. From New York Riis went to Jamestown, a small village in the northern part of the state, and there he spent the winter doing such trivial jobs as fell to him, glad to receive the small and irregular pay which enabled him to struggle on. For a time he worked in a Buffalo planing-mill. Summer found him working with a railroad gang outside the city. Then came the winter again, and with it work at good wages in a Buffalo shipyard. Destined to be known throughout the United States in later years for his social reforms, and his virile writings for the betterment of his fellow men, in these early days it was his knowledge of an honest trade that made it possible for him to build the foundations of future greatness.

Two years later Riis was back again in New York. Among the "want" advertisements, in a newspaper, his eye caught one which offered the position of city editor on a Long Island City weekly. The probability that a position thus advertised would be of small value was confirmed by the salary attached to it. Riis got the position; the salary was eight dollars a week, and at the end of two weeks the paper failed. Three wasted years they seemed; three years of no accomplishment.

Then came the turning. A former acquaintance, casually met, mentioned a job that was open in a news-gathering agency. "It is n't much — ten dollars a week to start with," he said. The brief two weeks' experience on the Long Island City paper had given Riis a slight familiarity with the requirements. In the shadow of Grace Church he prayed for strength to do the work which he had so long and so hardly sought. Beside him his dog, his only friend in these dark days, wagged his tail in encouragement. The die was cast.

The next morning Riis presented himself at the office of the New York News Association. The earnestness of the young man appealed to the desk editor, and despite his shabby clothes and thin, worn face, he was engaged. From that time on the path broadened and mounted steadily upward. He had begun his major lifework, a newspaper man.

A winter of hard work followed, but Riis kept his head and left no stone unturned to take every advantage of his opportunity. By day he gathered news about the city; by night he studied telegraphy. In the spring he took another step forward, and his conscientious work during the winter made it possible for him to meet the requirements of his post.

Some South Brooklyn politicians had started a weekly newspaper. They needed a reporter. Riis packed his grip and crossed the river. The new job paid fifteen dollars a week. And two weeks later he was made editor and his weekly pay was advanced to twenty-five dollars.

Then came another turning in the long, hard road. A letter from Denmark, from the little town of Ribe, from the fair-haired girl whom he had loved as a boy and for whom his love had grown through these lonesome years, told him that she loved him. A few months earlier this letter would have found him destitute, but now he was at the opening of his career. All things seemed possible. With redoubled enthusiasm he flung himself into his work.

By thrifty living Riis had saved seventy-five dollars. With this small sum and with notes for the balance, he bought the paper of which he was the editor.

11

He was determined to succeed. "The *News* was a big four-page sheet. Literally every word in it I wrote myself. I was my own editor, reporter, publisher and advertising agent. My pen kept two printers busy all week, and left me time to canvass for advertisements, attend meetings, and gather the news. I slept on the counter, with the edition for my pillow, in order to be up with the first gleam of daylight to skirmish for newsboys."

Once, impressed by the fervor of a preacher, he decided to throw up editorial work and take to preaching. "No, no, Jacob," said the preacher, "not that. We have preachers enough. What the world needs is consecrated pens."

That determined him, finally. He would pursue the vocation he had begun, but his pen would strive for the high ideal he had set before him.

Local politics were corrupt, and Riis with his paper began a campaign for reform. He was offered bribes; politicians urged him to cater to them for the rewards they could offer. Then, when nothing else could move him, they turned to violence. One cold winter night a gang of roughs called at his office. Riis was working late. One of the roughs, chosen by the others, entered the office with a club. A minute later Riis flung him through the front window of the office into the street. That ended the trouble.

In a few months Riis had paid in full the price of the newspaper and had established it firmly on its feet. But the months of cruel work had had their effect on him. He was badly overstrained. He needed a rest.

The doctors urged it. He knew they were right. With characteristic rapidity of determination, he sold the paper for five times what it had cost him, and with a snug sum in his pocket took the ship for Denmark to claim his bride.

It was no easy life in America to which he brought back his young wife. But in their small home they found in each other a peace and inspiration that made all things possible.

Eager always to try his hand at something new, Riis purchased a stereopticon and experimented with it in such small time as was left from his long day of newspaper activity and his domestic cares. It was to play a large part in his later life. "No effort to add in any way to one's stock of knowledge is likely to come amiss in this world of changes and emergencies, and Providence has a way of ranging itself on the side of the man with the strongest battalions of resources when the emergency does come."

For a long time after the sale of the Brooklyn paper Riis had tried to get a foothold on one of the New York dailies. His persistence was again rewarded and the position of a reporter on the *Tribune* was opened to him. Soon after came the recognition of his earnest and conscientious work in the form of an appointment to represent his paper at Police Headquarters. It was a hard and dangerous job, which required cool nerve and indefatigable energy. But of greater importance than the money that it paid, or the honor of the advancement, was the opportunity it afforded the young reporter to study at first-hand the conditions in which men and women lived in the congested tenements of the city — a study which placed at his hand the knowledge which later enabled him to become the champion of the slums.

The police reporter on a newspaper gathers and writes all the news that means trouble to someone — the fires, suicides, murders, and robberies. The *Tribune* office was in Mulberry Street, opposite Police Headquarters. All the rival newspapers had offices in the neighborhood, and among the reporters there was keen rivalry for news. Naturally, the police did not help, for to be "news" it must be discovered before it reached Police Headquarters, when all would know of it. Friendships and detective skill were important factors. Each reporter tried to be the first to get the news, write it up, and get it to his paper. There was lively competition among the reporters, for the man who got the news in print first had a "scoop" on his rivals.

Out of this busy life of the newspaper man, Riis now began to develop that interest which soon dominated his very existence; for from his daily contact with the daily life of the city slums he drew the inspiration to do his small part to better the conditions of the lives of those around him. Small as were his first efforts, there was soon inspired a veritable crusade in the soul of the Danish-American. Not as a newspaper reporter, not because he won his livelihood in the face of every difficulty, but because of his unselfish interest in his fellow men is Jacob Riis great among Americans.

One day he picked up a New York paper and saw

that the Health Department reported that during the past two weeks there had been a "trace of nitrates" in the city water. For months cholera, the dreaded scourge that comes from impure water and has, in the life of the world, killed more people than all the battles, had threatened the city. Riis investigated. The water supplying two million people must be pure. "Nitrates" were a sign of sewage contamination. The city was threatened, and no one seemed to realize the danger. The humble investigations of the newspaper reporter were to produce far-reaching results.

Riis wrote an article that day for the *Evening Sun*, and advised the people to boil the water before drinking it. Then, with a camera in his hand, he spent a week following to its source every stream that discharged into the Croton River. He found evidence enough: town after town discharged its sewage into the water which supplied New York City; people bathed in it; cities dumped refuse into it. With exact details, and the evidence illustrated with photographs, he returned.

The city was saved. So strong was the evidence that over a million dollars was promptly spent by the city to guard the water-supply. The real public-service life of Riis had begun.

In 1884, an awakened interest in the housing conditions in the tenement districts came to a head with the establishment of the Tenement-House Commission. It brought out the fact that the people living in the tenements were "better than the houses." Riis worked heart and soul for the cause. Four years later the reform was assured, with the backing of such men as Dr. Felix Adler and Alfred T. White. The Alder Tenement-House Commission was formed.

Now Riis turned to other conditions which cried aloud for reform. The "Bend" in Mulberry Street and the Police Lodging-Room system needed him. The "Bend" was a crowded slum that for a half-century had been the centre of vice and misery. Riis aroused the community, and in 1888 a bill was introduced in the Legislature to wipe it out bodily. To-day, a city park, a breathing-place and playground marks the site.

The Police Lodging-Room was another civic disgrace and a breeder of crime. In these vile and filthy rooms the Police Department gave night lodging to thousands of vagrants. The idea sounds well enough, but the system was wrong, and Riis realized it. In these foul quarters young men lodged with professional beggars and criminals, and learned the ways of vice; in these rooms was bred disease, physical as well as moral. Riis warned the city through his paper. Then his prophecies came true: typhus broke out in the Police Lodging-Rooms.

Slowly the force of Riis's newspaper articles made headway. One by one the rooms were closed. The Committee on Vagrancy was formed, of which Riis was a member; and the same year Theodore Roosevelt, later to be President of the United States, was appointed Police Commissioner. That was the end. The reform was accomplished. For the deserving poor, decent quarters were provided; the professional vagrants left the city.

In the gloom and dirt of the crowded tenements the souls of little children were shrunk and dwarfed. Riis was their crusader. Through his paper he appealed for flowers — flowers from those who came each day to the city from the country; flowers for "sad little eyes in crowded tenements, where the summer sunshine means disease and death, not play or vacation; that will close without ever having looked upon a field of daisies."

And the flowers came. Express wagons filled with them crowded Mulberry Street; people brought them in great armfuls. Little children, slovenly women, and rough men smiled and were glad. Riis brought God's country to Mulberry Street.

Then he turned his attention to the problem of child labor in the "East Factories" of New York. Only children over fourteen could be employed. But as there was no birth-registry, it could not be proved that thousands of little children quite evidently years under age were working there. Riis studied the problem. He found that certain teeth do not appear until the child is fourteen. He went to the factories and examined the children's teeth. His case was proved. With such evidence a committee was appointed and a correction of the wrong was begun.

"The Public School is the corner-stone of our liberties." The public schools of New York were crowded, the buildings were old, unsanitary, badly lighted, and many were actually dangerous fire-traps; dark base-

ments were used for playgrounds. There was in the
whole city but one school with an outdoor playground.
Worse yet, there were thousands of children who did
not go to school at all, and of those who did, conditions made truants of many.

Riis enlisted for this new battle. He took photographs, and gave lectures showing slides made from
his photographs, and he wrote constantly in the newspaper. Slowly the playgrounds came, and modern
school-buildings more adequate to house the city's
youth.

It is an endless list of public-service activities. In-
stigated by this foreign-born American, the reform of
the greatest American city was begun and carried far
along its way. Unfit tenements were torn down, parks
and playgrounds were established, the whole school-
system was remodeled, the old over-crowded prison
was condemned and a modern one erected, the civil
courts were overhauled; there was no end to his warfare on conditions which brought death and misery to
the city's poor.

A writer for a newspaper by vocation, Jacob Riis
found in his pen a strong power in his battles for reform. Throughout the latter years of his life he contributed frequent articles to magazines, and in 1890
published a book which alone will long make men remember the vital purpose of his life. *How the Other
Half Lives* tells by its title its message to the world; it
is the Golden Rule reduced to modern terms.

"I hate darkness and dirt anywhere, and naturally
want to let in the light . . . for hating the slum,

what credit belongs to me?" Unselfish, giving his all to the common cause, Jacob Riis is of the noble band of great Americans. As he lived, so he died, relatively a poor man. But poor only in worldly goods; for in the peace of his home and the love of wife and children he found a priceless wealth that gold can never buy. Many were his chances to profit by his work, but his creed was to give rather than to receive.

There were worldly honors that he received. There was the golden cross presented to him by King Christian of Denmark, and there were other recognitions to be found in the friendship and respect of the foremost citizens of the United States. But of all honors, the greatest was the affection of the thousands whom he helped a little nearer to the light, for whom he had opened windows in their souls.

No better advice has been given than this: "As to battling with the world, that is good for a young man, much better than to hang on to somebody for support. A little starvation once in a while, even, is not out of the way. We eat too much, anyhow, and when you have fought your way through a tight place, you are the better for it. I am afraid that is not always the case when you have been shoved through."

	DATE	
GAYLORD		